MANAGING CYBERSECURITY RISK

EDITION 3 – 2019

PUBLISHED BY
LEGEND BUSINESS BOOKS

EDITED BY
JONATHAN REUVID

Legend Business Ltd,
107-111 Fleet Street, London, EC4A 2AB
info@legend-paperbooks.co.uk | www.legendpress.co.uk

Print ISBN 9781789550528
Ebook ISBN 9781789550511
Set in Times. Printing managed by Jellyfish Solutions Ltd
Cover design by Simon Levy | www.simonlevyassociates.co.uk

CONTENTS LIST

FOREWORD

As one of the original contributors to what is now the third edition, it gives me enormous pleasure to contribute once again, albeit only by way of this foreword.

In fully acknowledging the threat and disruption caused by illicit/criminal cyber activities, I thought a short reflection on crime in general and the strain this causes to enforcement agencies globally would be helpful.

Terrorism, both national and international, continues and will remain for many years to come; knife and gun crime increases daily, fraud and cyber crime is at an all-time high, law enforcement acknowledges it can't cope and one UK force admits it writes off circa 45% of all crimes within 24 hours.

The need therefore to expand the accepted and established public/private partnerships is fundamental across the full spectrum of all preventative, investigative and private/public prosecutions. An open mind is required in order to support the enforcement agencies and the barriers of commerciality need to be crossed and diffused.

We need to maximise on the resources of those regulated security industry companies and personnel and find additional vehicles and empowerment to utilise their skills and, more importantly, their 24/7 presence.

In the arena of fraud and cyber – respecting the regulatory and data protection requirements – we must find acceptable ways of 'fast time' sharing information of suspected and actual perpetrators of these criminal activities.

If we accept this contention or, I would suggest, reality we must support those who are the victims of criminal cyber activities and authority in its prevention, detection and prosecution, plus of course the recovery of lost assets and business resumption. Applying this approach throughout the various chapters of this edition will identify areas of partnership to support each other, professionalise our response and make it harder and harder for those intent on causing cyber harm to achieve their objectives.

Initiatives for sharing and working together already exist at both national and international levels; the Global Cyber Alliance (GCA) and the Cyber Defence Alliance (CDA) are but two first-class examples.

Quoted recently was the need for more diversity across the world of cyber professionals. The 5-10 year need for circa 350,000 new persons in the industry and the requirement for an acknowledged educational pathway must be rectified.

The bad guys don't have our rules and associated costs, but together we can make their lives more difficult, more expensive, more punitive and difficult for them to succeed. On behalf of Jonathan and the team, our sponsors and authors, can I thank everyone for a structured, professional and practical third edition.

Don Randall MBE, CSyP

LIST OF CONTRIBUTORS

Mike Butler is CTO of Think Cyber Security Ltd. ThinkCyber apply learning and behavioural science in their software product RedFlags™ which delivers context sensitive and just in time security awareness training – find out more at www.thinkcyber.co.uk. Mike is an experienced IT and Information Security professional with more than 15 years' experience across the security, technology and telecommunications industries. Mike is a Certified Information Security Manager (CISM) and winner of the CISM worldwide achievement award. He holds a PhD in wireless communications and MSc in Communications Systems and Signal Processing.

Steve Durbin is Managing Director of the Information Security Forum (ISF). His main areas of focus include strategy, information technology, cybersecurity and the emerging security threat landscapes across both the corporate and personal environments. He has been ranked as one of the top 10 individuals shaping the way that organisations and leaders approach information security careers. Previously, he was senior vice president at Gartner.

Katherine Gibson is a Legal Director in the Employment Department in DLA Piper's London office. She has worked in-house for a number of years, initially working in an EMEA role for a global telecoms company and then in a UK role for a major global brand. Katherine moved back to private practice in March 2013, after almost six years in-house and now advises employers across both domestic and international employment and labour law matters. Katherine is experienced across all types of employment work from litigation to transactional support, including international project management. She advises employers across all sectors, particularly Transport, Hospitality and Leisure, Banking/Financial service and Life Sciences.

Chris Greany is the Head of Templar's EMEA Cyber Security Practice. Templar Executives is an award winning international cyber and information security consultancy. Recognised as an industry Thought Leader and solutions provider, it delivers a holistic approach to identifying, prioritising and mitigating business risk. Chris has successfully delivered enterprise risk security programs across the public and commercial sectors.

He is a member of the Cyber Security Advisory Board for the Institute of Asset Management and founding partner of the Global Cyber Alliance. Previously he was a member of the Bank of England's Cyber Security Board. At Barclays he headed the global insider threat program, building global security capabilities to address insider threats across the Group. He was also an advisor to government during the development of the UK's National Cyber Security Centre, part of GCHQ, which is the mainstay of the UK's national cyber security defences.

Marius Haak is an Associate in DLA Pipe's Frankfurt office and advises national and international companies on all issues of commercial criminal law. This includes both the representation of companies having suffered damage and those cases where employees committed offences to the alleged benefit of the company. His major focus is advising companies with regard to comprehensive internal investigations as well as the representation vis-à-vis investigating authorities and courts. Another area of focus is advising companies with regard to compliance issues, particularly in connection with the implementation, further development and verification of compliance systems/ anti-bribery-guidelines. He also supports clients with regard to criminal compliance due diligence in MAA processes. Marius also advises on the assertion of claims (for damages) in connection with criminal offences.

Armin Hendrich is a Partner based in DLA Piper's Vienna office and his practice focuses on the wider area of banking law including general and regulatory banking law, securities law, data protection law, compliance and regulatory (including outsourcing), anti-money laundering as well as sanctions regulations. Furthermore, he advises clients on corporate law, civil procedural law (including court hearings) and general rules of U.S. pre-trial disclosure in U.S. civil procedures and investigations of regulatory authorities in the intersection with civil code jurisdictions. He has accumulated expertise in air and space law and white collar crime. Armin has a strong background in IT and acts in the forefront of IT inclusion in legal processes. Building on his education and several years of experience he focuses on efficiency through legal project and process management. Armin manages several legal staff within the litigation & regulatory group and is part of DLA Piper's Service Delivery and Quality Group.

Dan Hyde is a Partner at Penningtons Manches Cooper LLP and Visiting Professor, School of Law, Queen Mary University of London. A pioneering cybersecurity lawyer, he identified cyberlaw as a distinct and developing area of law and put UK cybersecurity law on the map by writing the first professional reference book explaining what it was and how it could be applied to tackle the vast army of cyber threats and attacks. He has been instructed on a number of high profile cases and represents corporates and indivduals. An adviser to the Law Commission on cybersecurity legislation, Dan has lectured at esteemed institutions (University of London, Lloyds Underwriters and the Royal College of Surgeons) and is contributing editor of *Modern Financial Regulation*, a key professional reference work. His articles on cybercrime are published in the quality press and his commentaries broadcast on television and radio. *The Legal 500* describers him as "calm under pressure", "skilled at managing the crossover between parallel civil and criminal proceeding" and "a lawyer of the highest calibre".

Nick Ioannou is an IT professional, author and blogger with over 20 years' corporate experience, including 16 years using cloud/hosted software as a service (SaaS) systems. He started blogging in 2012 on free software and IT tips (nick-ioannou.com), currently with more than 450+ posts. His first book *Internet Security Fundamentals* currently available at www.booleanlogical.com is an easy to understand guide of the most commonly faced security threats and criminal scams aimed at general users.

Karla Reffold is the founder of BeecherMadden, with nominations for a number of awards for entrepreneurship. She is also a judge for the Cyber Security Awards. Karla has over 10 years' experience recruiting within information security. She is passionate about encouraging more women into the cyber security industry, improving the diversity of the industry, to help organisations build more successful teams. BeecherMadden recruits across the corporate governance sector, with offices in London, New York, Zurich and Singapore. While Karla specialises in senior appointments, BeecherMadden recruit from entry level upwards.

Maureen Kendal is Director of CyberCare Ltd which offers cyber security advice and support to individuals, families, business and organisations through helplines, clinics and training workshops. CyberCare offers training to local councils, schools and communities; charities tackling social care challenges such as vulnerable adults, human trafficking and domestic abuse, police, legal and social care services. Maureen is also an academic, educator and researcher. Previously at the Faculty of Computing and Digital Media at London Metropolitan University, she is currently a research and business associate at Ravenshoume University. She has memberships and fellowships: FRSA, FHEA, MBCS, OWASP. WITT and IMIS. Maureen's business interests are within innovative immersive virtual technologies, cyber security and cyber safety.

Richard Knowlton is Chairman of Richard Knowlton Associates, the security risk and resilience consultancy. He is a regular contributor to the media and at international conferences. Group Security Director of Vodafone 2009-2015, Richard worked earlier in Italy as Head of Security Global Operations with the UniCredit Group, the largest bank in Central and Eastern Europe. He is an honorary Life Member of the International Security Management Association (ISMA), and served on the board of the Consortium of the Commonwealth Cyber Crime Initiative.

Ross McKean is a partner in the London office of DLA Piper and is the joint head of the firm's UK data protection practice. Ross is recognised as a leading international technology lawyer and advises on global data governance and compliance, information security, breach response and global sourcing projects. His clients include organisations across a wide range of sectors including retail, financial services, technology, social media, digital advertising, e-commerce, B2C SaaS and life sciences. He also advises on contentious data protection and privacy matters including information access requests and privacy group actions.

Sam Millar graduated from Cambridge University (MA, Law) and the University of Illinois, USA (LLM, International and Comparative Law). He is a partner in the London office of DLA Piper and his practice focuses on Global Investigations. Sam has extensive experience in cross border regulatory and internal corporate investigations involving allegations of cyber crime, bribery, money laundering, market abuse, fraud and insider dealing. Sam has advised clients across sectors – including financial services and energy – on cyber crime and cybersecurity issues. He is on the FCA's Panel of Skilled Persons for s.166 FSMA reviews relating to conduct of business.

Chris Pinder works for IASME Consortium which is one of just five companies appointed as Accreditation Bodies for assessing and certifying against the government's Cyber Essentials Scheme. The Scheme focuses on the five most important technical security controls. These controls were identified by the government as those that, if they had been in place, would have stopped the majority of the successful cyber attacks over the last few years. Visit https://www.iasme.co.uk/ for more information.

Jan Pohle is a Partner in the Intellectual Property and Technology group of DLA Piper based in Cologne. He has experience in dealing with complex technology related projects and transactions such as strategic digitalisation, data privacy and cyber security matters. His practice is focused on strategic digitalisation and outsourcing projects (ITO and BPO) such as complex IT procurement and implementation projects involving the comprehensive legal structuring and management of such long-term projects. Jan further advises on international and domestic IT compliance, data privacy and cyber security projects and related ongoing support in this area. Finally, he deals with the legal management of (potential) cyberattacks. Jan is visiting lecturer at Humboldt University Berlin and the University of Oldenburg. He is, inter alia, co-editor of the benchmark publication *Computerrechtshandbuch* and author at Taeger/Gabel commentary on GDPR and BDSG.

Richard Preece is a "hybrid" consultant and leader, who connects business and technical leadership so that they can maximise the opportunities and minimise the risks of the Digital Age; in particular, by taking an integrated approach to make organisations more agile and resilient. Due to his work, he is a co-opted core member of the British Standard (BS31111) Cyber Risk and Resilience – Guidance for Top Management.

Don Randall is Chief Executive at Don Randall Associates and is currently a Senior Security Adviser to several major firms engaged in the following areas: cyber security, legal and regulatory, physical and technical security, international close protection, pre-employment screening, risk management, counter-terrorism, transnational criminal activities, asset recovery and fraud investigations.

Don is chairman of the 'Sister Banks', City of London Crime Prevention Association and 'Project Griffin' and a member of the City of London Crime Disorder Reduction

Panel. He is also a member of the London First Security Advisory Board, Executive Member of the London Resilience Business Sector Board and Co-founder and Vice-Chairman of the Cross Sector Safety & Security Communications initiative. Previously Don served with the City of London Police from 1969-1995, with specific emphasis on fraud and counter terrorism. Following 13 years at JPMorgan Chase as Managing Director, he joined the Bank of England in 2008 and was appointed the Bank's first Chief Information Security Officer in 2013. In 2007, Don was awarded an MBE for services to law enforcement for the harmonisation of the public/private sectors and has received a number of further awards since. He is a Fellow of the Security Institute and a Chartered Security Professional, and has also served as an external lay member of the City of London Police Committee.

Vijay Rathour is a partner at Grant Thornton UK LLP where he is Head of the Digital Forensics Group, overseeing and providing expert consultancy on a range of technological challenges. They include information governance; forensic evidence collection, recovery and review; incident response and data breach event handling; and structured and unstructured data collection and analysis. Vijay is a qualified solicitor and former barrister, having practised for over six years as a commercial litigator and the subsequent six years managing a digital risk and investigations boutique, overseeing some of the world's largest data breaches and forensic investigations. He enjoys a role on the Committee of the Cybercrime Practitioners Association and had been engaged by the Ministry of Justice to re-draft the Civil Procedure Rules on Electronic Disclosures and Investigative techniques for the modern era (CPR31 and PD31(B)). He also helped draft the investigation protocols used in the Technology and Construction Court.

Jonathan Reuvid is the editor in chief and a partner of Legend Business Books Ltd. A graduate of the University of Oxford (MA, PPE) he embarked on a second career in publishing in 1989 after a career in industry including Director of European Operations of the manufacturing divisions of a Fortune 500 multinational and joint venture development in China. Jonathan has more than 100 editions of some 45 titles to his name as editor and part-author. He is President of the Community First Oxfordshire charity.

Julian Richards is a Professor of Politics and Co-Director of BUCSIS, the Centre for Security and Intelligence Studies at the University of Buckingham. As well as teaching university programmes at various levels and supervising PhD research on all aspects of global security and intelligence issues, he is a frequent commentator in national and international media on security process and policy. Prior to academia, he had a long career at Government Communications Headquarters (GCHQ) fulfilling a variety of roles from analyst to manager and policy representative.

Christian Schoop is a partner in DLA Piper's Frankfurt office and advises national and international companies on all issues of criminal law and the monitoring of criminal investigations. This includes both the representation of companies having suffered damage and those cases where employees committed criminal offences to the alleged benefit of the company. A further focus of his work is on advising companies with regard to internal investigations and on the development and implementation of compliance systems. Furthermore, Christian monitors the conduct of compliance due diligence, particularly in the context of M&A transactions. In many cases, the advice also includes the involvement of international colleagues, e.g. from the U.S. or Great Britain. In addition to advising on traditional white-collar crimes such as corruption and breach of trust, Christian specialises in environment offences and offences related to cyber-attacks.

Jan Spittka is based in DLA Piper's Cologne office, where he is Counsel and advises domestic and foreign clients on all aspects of German and European law relating to privacy and data protection, cybersecurity and information technology. Jan has a special focus on privacy and data protection compliance with respect to the introduction of new technologies, international data transfers, cloud computing projects, processing of health data, breach notification and ePrivacy. He particularly advises on privacy and data protection as well as IT security requirements in the financial services and insurance sector and on enforcement activities of data protection authorities. A further focus of his work lies in the advice of outsourcing projects and legal questions arising from the Internet of Things and Industry 4.0.

Tim Ward is CEO and co-founder (with Dr. Mike Butler) of Think Cyber Security Ltd, who offer the next generation in Security Awareness. Tim has worked in IT for more than 20 years both in consulting and corporate IT with organisations including Logica, PA Consulting and Sepura, and was previouly Global Head of IT for the cyber division of BAE Systems (formerly known as Detica). He graduated with a First in Computer Sciences at the University of Leeds, holds an MBA from the Open University and a Post Graduate Diploma in entrepreneurship from Cambridge University.

Nick Wilding is General Manager of Cyber Resilience at AXELOS, a joint venture set-up in 2013 that is co-owned by Capita plc and the UK Government. AXELOS owns and nurtures a number of global best practice methodologies including ITIL®, PRINCE2® and RESILIA™ used by organisations in more than 150 countries to enable them to work and operate more effectively. Nick is responsible for RESILIA™ Global Best Practice, a portfolio of cyber resilience best practice publications, certified training, GCHQ certified cyber awareness training and leadership engagement tools designed to put the 'human factor' at the centre of cyber resilience strategy, enabling all your people to play their role in your organisational resilience.

INTRODUCTION

As Don Randall asserts in his foreword, the fight against cyber crime is a never-ending battle against resourceful criminals targeting all data and communications security from national defence and counter-espionage through to corporate business and personal online activity. What is more, we are not winning. As the incidence of cyber incidents increases remorselessly the best we can do is to contain the level of successful breaches; to do that we need to be fully aware of the sophisticated software, ever-evolving and mutating, which attackers employ. We also need to keep ourselves informed of the fraudulent techniques that invaders use to exploit our ignorance and penetrate our defences.

This third edition of *Managing Cybersecurity Risk* attempts to survey the battlefield, alert readers to the threats which they need to address, comment on their cultural implications and advise on managing the financial and social impacts of cyber incidents. Throughout the book there is a strong emphasis on training and achieving resilience.

There is a combiation of new contributors to this book with authors who have written for the title before and are updating and restating their analysis and advice. Among the former are Julian Richards of the University of Buckingham, whose opening chapter is a chilling account of the mega threats on the world stage, and Tim Ward of ThinkCyber, Steve Durbin of Information Security Forum and Chris Pinder of IASME Consortium who are each focused on aspects of human behaviour in terms of training and work culture.

Previous contributors are led by Nick Wilding of AXELOS RESILIA, sponsors of the title, who writes on the key role of training as the driver of behaviour change. He is supported by Karla Reffold on the retention of cybersecurity staff within an organisation, while the DLA Piper team provide advice on balancing information security good practice with the data protection and employment requirements. One year after its UK adoption, Dan Hyde of Penningtons reports on the current status of GDPR and the DPA.

Christopher Greany stresses the importance of securing companies from insider threats while Richard Knowlton reflects on the balance between cybersecurity risk and reward for small businesses. Nick Ioannou of Boolean Logical provides tutorials for us all on how to recognize and avoid the latest tricks and techniques that cyber criminals deploy to trap the unwary. The concluding chapter of the book is an authoritative dissertation on the social and financial impacts of cyber breaches provided by Vijay Rathour, leader of Grant Thornton's Digital Forensics Group.

I endorse fully Don Randall's thanks to all authors and sponsors of this new edition of *Managing Cybersecurity Risk* for their contributions and add my appreciation to Don himself for his return to the title of which he was a founding father.

Jonathan Reuvid
Editor

PART ONE

THE SCALE OF CYBER THREATS – TRAINING IS KEY

1

THE THREAT FROM BIG STATES

JULIAN RICHARDS, UNIVERSITY OF BUCKINGHAM

We might imagine that cyber threats from big states like Russia and China are primarily the concern of state intelligence agencies such as GCHQ and MI5. This, however, is the wrong way to look at the situation. Due to increasingly blurry lines between activists, criminals and states, everyone now needs to think about the threat from the big state actors, from governments to businesses, large and small.

In this chapter, I will begin by considering which state actors are the ones to worry about. We will consider their objectives in the cyber threat landscape; the complex array of actors involved; the effects their actions have on a range of organisations; and the key messages we should take away in conclusion.

STATES POSING CYBER THREAT

Taking a Western perspective on the situation, there is no doubt that Russia and China continue to pose a substantial and constantly evolving cyber threat to the interests of a number of states and their allies. Both of these states have a strong interest in developing their hostile cyber capabilities, for a range of strategic political and economic reasons. Both will increasingly seek to appear at the cutting-edge of cyber threat technology and capability, and will aim to be leading players in cyberspace. There is also mounting evidence that Russia in particular – or at least forces sympathetic to it – is engaged in comprehensive information warfare against the West and its citizens using industrialised cyber techniques.

But these are not the only states to worry about. Latterly, Iran has shown a growing capability, primarily driven by its animosity towards the West (and Israel) for supporting crippling sanctions on the Iranian economy. North Korea – to whom the 2017 Wannacry attack has been partially attributed – also considers itself to be locked in an existential conflict with the West. From time to time, other state players will appear on the scene. Examples include the shadowy Syrian Electronic Army, which directed cyber attacks primarily against the West in the early years of the Syrian civil war. Israel is also emerging as a very capable cyber power, albeit focusing its attention very firmly on state and non-state foes in its immediate region, such as Hamas and Hizbollah. Future conflicts and geopolitical crises may see other, unexpected state actors appear on the scene.

MOTIVATIONS FOR STATE CYBER ATTACKS

There are a number of complex and interlocking reasons for how and why big states may wish to become involved in hostile cyber activity. The most important of these is a general feeling in rival states that the West – and particularly the US – exercise a hegemonic dominance not only in the global economy, but specifically in the global internet architecture. This is not without reason. US corporations substantially dominate global internet architecture, products and services. As the internet was invented in the US, it has shaped the governance and processes underpinning the global system, such as ICANN and DNS arrangements, and internet protocol configurations. As aspiring major global players with an interest in reducing the dominance of the US, both China and Russia see cyberspace as a key area of battle for major power status.

Related to this is a clear realisation that the major Western military and intelligence agencies, headed by the Pentagon and NSA in the US, have made cutting-edge cyber capabilities very much at the centre of their activities and operations. Within NATO, the UK is clearly not far behind, helped in part by its strong and historical connection with the US. China and Russia feel they have no choice but to match these cyber powers if they are to compete on the world stage.

Aspiring world power status is not the only driver, however. In some cases, the big states will seek to disrupt, undermine and even "punish" those who attempt to stand in their way. This was partly the case with the NotPetya attack on Ukraine in 2017. Here, organisations tangentially connected to Ukrainian companies became caught in the crossfire. This included disruption to supply networks, and direct disruption of information and services. There is also much evidence that Russia in particular has been behind information attacks and industrialised "fake news", attempting to influence Western opinion against its own governments and to sow discord and distrust across Europe and NATO.

It is the case that, along with hackers more generally, the big states will sometimes be testing exploits in the marketplace to see how they work and the effects they could have. Wannacry, again, could have been partially a case of this on the part of the North Koreans. In a sense, it could have been the cyber equivalent of a ballistic missile test.

One of the most important drivers for Russia and China particularly is a strong desire to modernise their military capability. Both of these states realise that their capabilities are still remarkably small when compared to NATO and the US. Both are also acutely aware that history has caused their militaries to lag badly behind their Western foes technologically. There is one key solution to this: massive and organised theft of the latest military technologies, so that years of industrial neglect can be leapfrogged.

Cyber penetrations offer huge opportunities for industrial and commercial espionage and theft. A dragnet policy on information is deployed, collecting as much as possible from every available source, whether overt or covert, and then sifting through for the nuggets of technological advantage. Industrial-scale and automated attacks on commercial and government networks using APTs will constantly scan for breaches in the wall, through which information can be exfiltrated. And businesses need to think laterally here in terms of supply-chains. While the ultimate targets may be the big company and government networks, back-door accesses through contractors and suppliers will offer a myriad of opportunities. Think of the recent problems with CCleaner or MeDoc, which typified upstream software exploits. Think, also, of old-fashioned insider approaches, of which there have been several examples recently in governmental and student environments.

CYBER THREAT ACTORS

It is important not to think of hostile states in cyberspace as isolated actors. Instead, cyberspace is a complex ecosystem comprising states, criminals, hacktivists, terrorists, and straightforward hacking hobbyists. Each will interact with others in a variety of circumstances, whether it is buying stolen information, observing or stealing techniques, or supporting ideological and strategic objectives. In many hostile states, patriotic hackers will do the work of the intelligence services, either through a sense of duty, or through back-door contracts and commissions. Very often the connection between a state and a hacking group is deliberately opaque. In many cases, money will motivate the sale of an exploit, the undertaking of a particular penetration, or the obtaining of sensitive data. The arrangement suits everyone: the big states can deny accountability, while the attackers make financial and reputational profit.

The former Yahoo CEO has squarely accused Russian intelligence agents of being behind at least some of the massive data breaches that Yahoo suffered in 2013. More recently, a report by Symantec that the hacking group Buckeye had been using NSA-developed exploits targeting Microsoft Windows for commercial espionage, suggested that the tools had been obtained a couple of years earlier by Chinese intelligence and "repurposed". Meanwhile, a report on Operation Cloud Hopper, investigating APT10's cyberespionage attacks against managed service providers (MSPs) in the global network, suggests the group is "closely aligned with Chinese strategic interests".[1] In other words, APT10 are almost certainly working for or with the Chinese state to effect industrial-scale cyberespionage, but the compromises against MSPs in the core network have the potential to affect a huge number of organisations with collateral damage to data integrity. In these examples we can see the fluidity between states and

1. PWC UK and BaE, "Operation Cloud Hopper" (April 2017):
https://www.pwc.co.uk/cyber-security/pdf/cloud-hopper-report-final-v4.pdf

other hacking actors in cyberspace. And Western agencies such as NSA unwittingly find themselves in the mix over time, adding weight to the "fire and forget" nature of modern cyber capabilities.

EFFECTS AND CONSEQUENCES

The message that emerges from this landscape for organisations across the globe is that, while the big state actors will have particular strategic motivations for carrying out cyber attacks or information operations, the fluidity and complexity of the cyber threat are such that a myriad of effects will follow. In their relentless pursuit of information of potential commercial and military advantage, the big states will think about attack surfaces and penetrations in the widest possible sense. This means that any network connectivities could offer opportunities, whether these are in core network architecture, in MSPs or other supplier nodes, or in the expanding range of devices and systems connecting to the internet. (And on this front, they will think about opportunities from the deployment of such equipment all the way back to its construction in the workshop. This may have been how Stuxnet was delivered, for example.)

This is one of the particular worries around the IoT, especially where evidence suggests that more than half of new smart devices are currently installed without changes to factory settings. It is also the logic behind the panic over Huawei's 5G architecture. The suggestion is that the company – either directly or through back-door penetration by the Chinese state – may build weaknesses and compromises into the system in such a way that they can be called upon at some time in the future to exfiltrate information, enable a penetration, or "switch off the lights". Whether this is a realistic fear or the stuff of science fiction is very hard to determine at the present time, but it certainly needs thinking about.

It is also the case that the big states may be piggy-backing on criminal or activist activity, whether to hide their authorship of particular attacks or through marriages of convenience with non-state threat actors. The big states will also be closely monitoring the effect of particular exploits or approaches by way of seeing what works and what does not; and might be occasionally throwing particular exploits out to see what effect they may have. The latter might be a particular threat from the smaller and less sophisticated states such as North Korea or Syria.

For companies and organisations, the result is that damage can be suffered to data or system integrity, and indeed to reputation, even if the company in question was far from being the main target in mind. The evolution of APTs and related industrialised and automated attacks such as DDOS-for-hire and business email compromise (BEC) will all be considered as methods for harvesting data by the big states, and will be attacks in which there will be a lot of collateral damage. In this sense, some have equated cyber weapons to gas attacks: you never know where the gas will drift and cause casualties.

CONCLUDING THOUGHTS

The big state intelligence agencies such as NSA and GCHQ (through the NCSC) will clearly have big states such as China and Russia very firmly in their sights. Such foes will generally be at the big and sophisticated end of the spectrum, able to undertake attacks of a size and complexity that would normally be beyond the reach of smaller groups such as criminals or terrorists. In many cases, all the big states will be playing something of a cat-and-mouse game with each other, trying to spot and learn from each other's techniques and capabilities.

However, a number of recent incidents highlight a complex cross-fertilisation of big state actors and a myriad of other cyber threat actors, large and small. Cyber spies and attackers may be lurking amongst hacktivists, criminals and terrorists, sometimes deliberately so in order to evade detection. This means that all organisations need to be alive to the threats to systems and data, wherever they may come from and however they may be motivated.

NCSC cannot protect us completely from all of these threats, but their advice is the same as for all threats. All companies and organisations need to take basic cybersecurity seriously and to make their systems as resilient as possible. Particular vulnerabilities may be situated in configurations of internet connections, and particularly the expansion of such connections with the ever-expanding pool of internet-enabled technologies and devices. Protection of data in and via the cloud is also an area of concern. If you leave the door open, all sorts of people may come through.

With the insider threat still a surprisingly resilient aspect of cybersecurity, initial and ongoing vetting of staff remains a very important area of security. This will be particularly the case for any suppliers or contractors to government (and not just to defence or security – think back doors again). In all of these areas, organisations would do well to follow NCSC's advice closely, and to make sure they have good and updated access to strategic threat intelligence.

In closing, it is worth considering a small note of caution in all of this. It is the case that not everyone agrees with the more cataclysmic assessments of Chinese and Russian cyber activity. As with "revisionist" theories of the Cold War, the Russians and Chinese may be just as worried about us as we are about them. There is also the "economic interdependency" argument, articulated recently in a study by the Harvard Belfer Center[2]. This suggests that China in particular may not wish to substantially undermine and attack Western networks, even if they had the capability to do so, as the ensuing economic and political chaos would affect their economy as much, if not more, than ours. On the information manipulation front, there are also a number of recent academic analyses which suggest that attempts to influence voters and elections through manipulative use of news and social media, are probably much less effective and influential than we might sometimes imagine.

All of these notes of caution carry logic. But at the same time, the dragnets for information being deployed by the big states will catch many on the margins, and it is generally better to be safe than sorry.

---

2. Jon R. Lindsay, "Exaggerating the Chinese Cyber Threat". Policy Brief, May 2015

2

THE GDPR AND DPA 2018

DAN HYDE, PENNINGTONS MANCHES COOPER LLP

INTRODUCING THE UK REGIME

The General Data Protection Regulations ("the GDPR") came in to force in all European Union member states on 25 May 2018 and were brought in to effect here in the UK by the Data Protection Act 2018 (DPA). Whilst the references in this chapter will be to the GDPR it should be noted that this is shorthand because, for a comprehensive understanding of the position, one should need to have regard to the combined provisions of the GDPR and DPA. The aim of this chapter is to take the hard work out of such an exercise by setting out the key provisions and concepts such that the reader is introduced to what the legislation primarily requires.

The first question that needs answering is whether the GDPR applies to your business. It should be noted that the GDPR has extra-territorial effect so that it applies not only to UK businesses but to all businesses offering goods or services in the European Union or monitoring individuals in the European Union. The UK is still (at the time of writing) within the EU and the GDPR applies whether or not the business has any branch or office in the EU or indeed any server. In short the GDPR will apply to most if not all businesses that have an EU customer base. This is because it focuses on the protection of the European individual's data wherever that data may be. The best question to ask yourself then is whether your business handles the personal information of EU individuals?

Once you have decided whether the GDPR will apply to your business, you next need to understand the important concepts in GDPR and data protection. The first of these is '*data processing*'. Any operation performed on personal data such as collection, recording, organising, structuring, storage, adaptation, retrieval, consultation, use, disclosure by transmission, making available or transferring, disseminating or deleting will constitute data processing. Virtually any action in relation to personal data will constitute data processing. Data processing is governed by the GDPR which stipulates when this can be conducted lawfully (see post). The '*data subject*' is the person the data is about, for example a customer or patient is a data subject when their personal data is processed for a purpose of the business. We will look at some of the legitimate purposes later in this chapter. Of particular importance is the '*data controller*'; this is the person or entity (whether public or private) that collects and processes the personal data. The controller determines the purposes and means of processing personal data and has extensive obligations under the GDPR. Finally '*personal data*' means exactly that, data which relates to any identifiable person who can be directly or indirectly identified by reference to an identifier. This definition is wide as even personal data that has been pseudonymised or anonymised can fall within the scope of the GDPR if the true identity of the individual can be determined from the data in question; this then will depend upon how difficult or possible it is to identify the particular individual despite the use of the pseudonym or anonymous title. In summary, GDPR will apply to personal information (widely defined) and will govern the actions of the controllers and processors of that personal information (very widely defined).

LEGAL OBLIGATIONS

The GDPR places legal obligations on both controllers and processors and general principles that run through GDPR must be applied. The general principles are:

- *Lawful fairness and transparency* – data has to be processed in accordance with EU and member state laws and data controllers have to be transparent with customer information regarding what happens to their personal data. Handling personal information and a legitimate way and ensure there is a transparency as to how that personal data is handled is at the heart of GDPR.
- *Purpose limitation* – the data has to be collected for a specific explicit and legitimate purpose. It cannot be used for other purposes beyond that specific explicit legitimate purpose. What is legitimate will be looked at in this chapter.
- *Data minimisation* – you should only request information that is required and relevant for the purpose for which the data is being collected. This is the de minimis rule so that the data controller should only request the minimum amount of information that is needed for the specific explicit legitimate purpose.
- *Accuracy* – data controllers must ensure that their data is accurate. If not it should be rectified and reasonable steps should be taken that it is accurate. The data must be kept up to date and every reasonable step should be taken to ensure that it is accurate having regards to the purpose for which it is being processed and where inaccuracies are discovered data should be erased or rectified without delay.
- *Limited storage* – data should only be stored for a limited period and except for

archiving and scientific research purposes it should not be stored beyond the life of the specific explicit and legitimate purpose.

- *Integrity and confidentiality* – data has to be processed in a matter that minimises the risk to the confidentiality and integrity of the data. This should include protection against unlawful or unauthorised processing or accidental damage or loss.
- *Accountability* – the data controller must be seen to be accountable. This means you must be in a position to prove that the general principles are being applied and that the burden of proof is on the data controller to show this is the case.

In order to process personal information, you must identify a legitimate reason for doing so, otherwise the processing will not be lawful under the GDPR. The legitimate reason that is relied upon must be documented.

There must then be a legitimate purpose (lawful basis) for processing personal data and these are as follows:

1. That you have the consent of the data subject. This is dealt with in detail later but it will be essential to document that the consent has been given.
2. That processing is necessary for the performance of a contract with a data subject or to take steps to enter into a contract. This then is the contractual purpose.
3. That processing is required to comply with a legal obligation. This then is the legal obligation the data controller must meet and that the processing is necessary to protect the vital interest of a data subject for another person.
4. That processing is necessary to protect the vital interests of the data subject or another person.
5. That the processing is necessary for the performance of a task in the exercise of official authority vested in the controller or something that is in the public interest.
6. That the processing is necessary for the legitimate interest of the controller or a third party. This then will include the commercial interests of the controller as such interests are capable of being a legitimate interest. The test is whether the interest of the controller is overridden by the interests, rights or freedoms of the data subject. A balance needs to be performed to ensure that where legitimate business interests that are pursued they are not overtaken by the interests, rights and freedoms of the data subject whose personal information is being used for the purpose.

It is important to select the most appropriate lawful basis for processing; if for example, the legitimate purpose relied upon is the consent of the data subject, there will be problems if in due course the data subject withdraws their consent. With this in mind, it is advisable to choose and document, where possible, another legitimate interest as that avoids the situation where the consent is later withdrawn or cannot be demonstrated, and the controller is left holding information which has no lawful basis.

EXPLICIT REQUEST REQUIREMENTS

There are, however, special categories of data where explicit consent of the data subject will be required. Personal data that is categorised as special category personal data will require a higher hurdle in order to justify its processing is legitimate. Special category personal data is any data that reveals racial or ethnic origin, political opinion, religious or philosophical beliefs, trade union membership or genetic data, biometric data for the purpose of identifying a person or data concerning health or data concerning a person's sex life or sexual orientation. Should you seek to process this sort of data then, under the GDPR this is prohibited unless the data subject has given explicit consent to its processing for one or more specified purpose(s). There are limited exceptions to this; for example, where the processing is necessary to protect the vital interests of the data subject or another person where the data subject is physically or legally incapable of giving consent or where the processing relates to personal data which has manifestly been made public by the data subject and is thus in the public domain already, but exceptions will be of limited application. There is a further exception for processing where it is necessary for the purposes of preventative or occupational medicine or management of health or social cares systems and services pursuant to a contract with a heath care professional. This exception will only apply to the healthcare and occupational medicine arena, ancillary uses such as health insurance will not fall within it and explicit consent will be required.

To constitute explicit consent there must be unambiguous consent to the use of the special category data. This must be an affirmative action by the data subject with demonstrable proof that explicit unambiguous consent to the use of the data was given. This means an act that has been freely given and is a clear indication of the client's agreement to the processing of their personal data. Where there is a significant difference in power between the data subject and controller, such as between an employee and employer, it will likely be presumed that consent was not feely given. Silent or inactive consent, such as a pre-ticked box, would also not be considered as consent, although a box which has been deliberately ticked would suffice as that would indicate active consent so long as there was proper information as to the use the data was to be put to.

The key here is to remember that the burden of proof is with you and that you need to show that the consent given was informed, intelligible and easily accessible. It should be expressed in clear and plain language and be distinguishable from other matters. A signed form that includes a number of other matters would fall foul of this unless the consent to the use of the personal information could be clearly identified and understood. It should also be plain that any customer was informed before giving consent that they were able to withdraw it and that children (in the UK this is defined as below 13) have parental consent as otherwise their data cannot be lawfully processed.

PERSONAL DATA COLLECTION

In order to be transparent and comply with the GDPR, when a data controller collects the personal information form the data subject they have to give, at the time they collect the health data, the following information:

1. The identity of the contact person or data controller;
2. The purpose for which the data is being processed;
3. The period for which the data will be stored (this can be an estimate at the outset);
4. If it is intended to transfer the data to another country;
5. If the business would wish to process the customer data for another secondary purpose in addition to the specific explicit purpose that have been given; and
6. Explain the data subject's rights, namely:
   a. That they have the right to be kept informed and to access their own personal data and these are fundamental rights, and that they have a right to data portability so that they can transfer data from one data controller to another.
   b. That they have the right to object to the processing of their data.
   c. That they have the right to request rectification of their data if it is inaccurate or incomplete.
   d. That they have the right to deletion of their data, known as the right to be forgotten. This might apply where a data subject has withdrawn consent and no other lawful basis remains that can justify the storage or processing or that the principles of limited storage and data minimisation support the request for deletion.
   e. That they have a right to restrict the processing of their data.
   f. That they have also rights in relation to any automated processing and profiling.

It is important to note these rights, the rights of the individual, are at the very core of the GDPR and organisations should strive to ensure they can document their application. In practical terms, you will need to implement internal policies that ensure all the key information is documented; this will ensure you record the legitimate lawful basis for processing and where consent is relied upon it is properly recorded. In relation to special category data the record will need to demonstrate explicit consent.

Businesses will be required to designate an independent and appropriately skilled Data Protection Officer (DPO) were the organisation is a public body or where the core activities involve regular and systematic monitoring of personal data on a large scale or the processing of special categories of data or large scale processing of sensitive data. The likelihood is that unless your business crunches significant amounts of personal or sensitive information as its primary activity then it will not be forced to designate a DPO, if the activity is secondary or ancillary this requirement should not bite. That said, in the light of the burdens of recording and accountability brought by the GDPR organisations should carefully consider appointing a DPO where funds allow and the role would otherwise eat in to the time of other personnel.

GDPR IN CASES OF DATA BREACH

The GDPR is also a game changer in the event of a data breach. There will be mandatory notification of a cyber-security breach to the supervisory authority without undue delay and, in any event, in no later than 72 hours if there is a risk to individuals rights and freedoms. This will nearly always apply unless encryption or other defence mechanisms has kept the data absolutely intact and uncompromised. Where a report is late, then a reasoned justification for the delay must be justified. This all then goes back to the raison d'etre of the GDPR, the protection of the individuals' data rights; a risk in relation to their rights and freedoms must be notified to the Information Commissioners Office (ICO) and, if there is a high risk to the individuals' rights or freedoms, then they too must be notified. There is then a dual test: a minor risk requires notification to the ICO; a high risk requires additional notification to the individuals whose personal information has been affected. There are very limited exceptions to this, such as where encryption or other protection is in place, but in such a situation there would not be high risk. The other is where individual notifications would be disproportion and a public information campaign or other method might better meet the need to inform.

Failures in relation to notification of breaches can be fined the greater of 10 million euros or 2% of worldwide annual turnover for the preceding financial year. Other breaches could be double that and the greater of 20 million or 4% of worldwide annual turnover. Those sums are the maximums and we will need to watch how the ICO pitches the level of these fines as, to date, most of the investigations were commenced and sanctions imposed under the previous pre-GDPR regime because the initial failures arose whilst the old law was still in force. It is important to understand however that the threat to your business will come not only from the regulator's fines but from those individuals who may sue individually or together (in what is termed a class action) where their personal information has not been safeguarded and where a breach of the GDPR can be identified. The classic example is where, following a cyber-attack, customers' personal data is compromised. The consequent investigation by the regulator can lead to adverse findings and fines that are then seized upon by the customers (whose data was compromised) to found an action against the organisation.

Under the old law it has been held by UK courts that even where the breach (cyber-attack) is caused deliberately by a disgruntled rogue employee seeking to harm the business that business (as the employer) is liable to those customers' whose personal data has been compromised. The expectation is that this will continue to apply under the current law and businesses will be even more exposed as, pursuant to the GDPR, breaches will need to be notified. That notification will increasingly result in the regulator putting the business under the microscope and consumers becoming aware where their personal information is at risk and the business found to be at fault. In short there has never been a better time to ensure that your business is in GDPR order and that you are dealing with your customers' personal data in a compliant manner. You should always be ready demonstrate that you have a legitimate purpose and that you deal with personal data in accordance with the GDPR principles.

3

DRIVING SECURITY BEHAVIOUR CHANGE THROUGH MOMENTS THAT TRULY MATTER

NICK WILDING, GENERAL MANAGER, CYBER RESILIENCE, AXELOS RESILIA

A CISO at a London based organisation recently said to me: "It's all about giving our people the confidence to know what they need to do and to make it easy for them to do the right things." It sounds easy, doesn't it.

Organisations increasingly understand that they need all their employees to play their role in enterprise-wide cyber resilience. Sadly, all too often our employees don't know what their role is or what is entailed in playing their role. There's also an inherent challenge – as a recent paper that assessed the challenges of communicating security to employees in media organisations stated:

> *"It is now a cliché to observe that the key to security is people. 'Human factors' are routinely cited by cyber security experts as the number one line of defence – or, more commonly, of weakness. The discussion of those humans is often tinged with frustration and despair. People, it is sometimes suggested, are what cause well-made security plans to come unstuck."*

Our people are often still regarded as part of the problem rather than an integral part of an enterprise wide cyber resilience strategy and response. Too often organisations pay lip service to 'training' their people, relying on outdated annual 'tick-box' training that has no impact on secure behaviours.

Marketing communications 101 tells us that you must reach the right people with the right messages at the right time to stand the best chance of that message being heard and/or acted upon.

The problem we typically see in achieving sustained security behaviour change in organisations is that this simple fact is so often ignored. Security awareness training is usually not well targeted, it's poorly communicated and usually positioned as 'mandatory training'. Do it and do it now. We're fighting against normal human behaviour – people don't like being told to 'do training'. It's as if training is being 'done to us' and that we're trying to programme our people in the way we programme computers to do the right thing at the right time. We have no choice or say in how we would like to learn.

As Tim Ward highlights later in Chapter 8 of this book, behaviour change typically is not sustained without the appropriate personal motivation, the ability to make the change easily and the necessary prompts to make the change.

Gone are the days where we believe that 'tick-box' security awareness training will enhance our security controls or sustain vigilant behaviours. We need new evidence based approaches to training for behaviour change. Changing our security behaviours in the workplace can take time and 'time means money'. What does an effective approach look like and how can we work towards making security behaviours habitual and seamless across our 'business as usual' operations.

ESSENTIAL BEHAVIOUR CHANGE TECHNIQUES

This short chapter is designed to provide five essential techniques for driving behaviour change through moments that truly matter.

1. Keep it regular: leadership, communication and language is everything

> *"It's not the end of the world. If something happens, it happens."*

This was a comment made by an 'average technology user' in research carried out by the National Institute of Standards and Technology (NIST) in the US. They assessed perceptions and beliefs about cybersecurity and online privacy, and identified that consumers are increasingly desensitized to cyber risks.

The quote highlights the difficulties we face in moving beyond the frustration, weariness and 'security fatigue' many of us feel from the bombardment of messages about the dangers lurking online. We're tired of being told the sky is falling down. But the risk of cyber-attack remains real and relentless – both at home and in the workplace. The reality is that cyber attackers often find it easier to communicate with, engage and influence the behaviours of our employees than we do.

People need to hear from their leaders. Information security is a business risk and leadership teams have a vital responsibility to show their commitment and dedication to leading the way in protecting what's most precious and valuable to them. The goal is to be able to say "That's the way we do things around here". The active and continued involvement of leaders - being seen and heard - in their organisations' Information Security training campaigns will be time well spent. Leaders must also appreciate that they're far from immune to attack themselves – sharing their own stories can be a powerful way to encourage and engage their workforce to do the right thing.

2. Keep it real and relevant: the irresistible power of stories and language

Jim Baines valued his business, Baines Packaging. He started it nearly 30 years ago in Peekskill, New York, and is currently its CEO. British born, Jim is driven, innovative, and values transparency. He never knew he was a 'whale' until he did something careless. Something he admits now was 'stupid' - he opened an attachment sent by someone he hardly knew, but who seemed credible. That casual error almost ruined his business, and his life.

Are you hooked? You should be. It's a story we're all familiar with. Any one of us could have done what Jim did, to find ourselves in his position — at the nexus of a crisis the outcome of which is maddeningly uncertain. If we're drawn to him, to his story, and the reasons why he fell into the trap set by hackers, it's perhaps because we don't want to look, but find it difficult to look away.

That's the power of a good story. I believe it can, and should, be used to help us fight cybercrime and boost our resilience to attacks. In fact, it's one of the most efficient and effective ways of doing so. Why? Because telling stories is fundamental to our humanity. Stories help us make sense of the world, to better understand its threats and opportunities, so we can mitigate the former and recognise and harness the latter.

Simply put, our imaginations are what drive us. All the technical knowledge in the world, all the planning and analysis won't help if, fundamentally, you don't understand the essence of a threat nor have an emotional investment (individually, collectively) in dealing with it. That's what stories enable. They deal with human feeling, not jargon. They focus on broad but fundamental outcomes, and they drive action. That's the vital element: if you *feel* you need to act then you probably *will*. If you merely think about it, you might delay doing what's necessary to protect what you value until it's too late.

The author Maya Angelou famously wrote: "I've learned that people will forget what you said, people will forget what you did, but people will never forget how you made them feel." And what's the best way to get that emotional connection? – by telling stories.

Cybersecurity risks are so often reported as a set of statistics or technical jargon… data about the latest threats, the changing techniques adopted by cyber attackers and the number of events and incidents experienced. As a method of bringing about systemic and cultural change, this is a flawed approach.

Great stories can help to demystify and to highlight exactly what role we can all play in greater resilience. Jim Baines couldn't agree more: "Unwitting is the point. Some of my friends say 'witless' but that's another matter. The point is, we were complacent. We thought it was a technical not a human issue. But it's all about the human and how we make sure they are part of the solution not blamed for mistakes that anyone can make."

Read more about Jim Baines in *'Whaling for Beginners'* a CEO cyber thriller published by RESILIA.

3. Keep it timely: training to the right people in the right place at the right time

When can training be most effective in driving new behaviours? When it's delivered to the right person, with relevant content at the time that person has an immediate training need.

Training should be aligned with tasks that employees perform as part of their job. Different cyber-attacks can target particular functions and people within organisations. Take Payment Diversion Fraud or CEO spear phishing for example – these are typically targeted at those in finance, accounts payable and related roles. In trying to make them more aware and vigilant, build training and communication programmes that talk to them and use scenarios and stories they can relate to.

You can also provide hints, tips and nudges direct to people and teams that have a specific message relating to their role and potential vulnerability to an attack. These can be provided in the working environment as you're carrying out your job.

4. Keep it fresh and varied: we value choice and we need digital skills

The ability for organisations to manage and influence employees' security behaviours will be influenced by how the employees want to learn, at home and at work. We are now all bombarded with and consume information at all times of the day. This has made us all the more demanding in what we want to see and how we want to 'engage' with information. We also all engage with and learn from different training techniques in different ways. Varied content, ideally developed and designed with the involvement of your employees is critical to success. This means corporate training has had to 'up its game' over the last few years to meet our changing training appetites.

Add to this the perceived complexity of cyber security and most people's only passing interest in what it means for them and cyber security behaviour change can often be seen as an unattainable goal. Yet every one of us can be a target – in the home and 'on the move' as much as at work. All too many of us have been personal victims of cyber-crime attacks or have been 'one click' away from disaster. Our digital skills need to be 'tuned and retuned' to the ever changes threats and techniques used to trick us.

Content will always be king. Develop compelling training that make the risks real and which immerse the learner in fun and compelling ways. Combine different training techniques like games, animations, stories and simulations with tests, competitions, surveys and active involvement of your employees will pay dividends. Your employees are your people on the frontline – they have the experience, the 'water-cooler' conversations, the ideas and enthusiasm that can transform your campaign. Develop them as your team of evangelists and advisers for how to build the digital skills across the organisations.

Look to work with your positive cynics and outliers – the people who can sometimes be those who ignore 'corporate' training. They can bring their own perspectives and ideas if given the appropriate motivation and incentive to be involved.

5. Keep it short: the power of microlearning

We all forget stuff very quickly – typically we can forget 80% of what we learn in 30 days. We also have increasingly short attention spans and demand training that's interesting and relevant.

Short focused 'bitesize' learning designed to meet a specific learning outcome available on multiple devices can help transform your cyber awareness training programme. The good news is that there are strategies that can be used to improve memory retention. There are two primary factors:

• *Repetition:* the more frequently we repeat something, or provide complementary reminders, the more likely it is to stick in our minds. For cyber awareness learning, this means effectiveness is directly correlated to regular, ongoing updates, refreshers and reminders, which use varied techniques like animations, games, real use-cases, lunch and learn sessions, competitions etc. to engage and encourage our employees to talk openly about their experiences.

• *Quality of meaning*: long-term retention and adoption is also dependent on the relevant, meaningful connections you can make between the new information and the things you already know. This is where stories and narrative are vital in making learning relevant and engaging, weaving cyber awareness into everything we do at home, in the workplace and on the move.

For the learner micro-learning can be highly targeted and provide that much required reminder to reinforce key cyber awareness messages and campaigns. For the organisation well designed, bitesize learning provides affordable and agile training that can be easy and cost effective to update to ensure the training stays up to date and relevant.

IN SUMMARY

Returning to the CISO who said to me recently: "It's all about giving our people the confidence to know what they need to do and to make it easy for them to do the right things", I hope these five points have provided some insight into how cyber security behaviours can become part of the culture of an organisation.

Cyber threats represent a systemic business risk to organisations which need to manage and measured effectively. Our employees should play a significant part in any organisations response to a risk that is only going to become more pervasive. We need new approaches to listening to and motivating all our people to want to do the right thing – to help them understand and act securely to the digital risks they face at work and at home. New approaches to balancing the right amount of training where and when it's needed most and new approaches to creating real engagement in information security.

We have an organisational responsibility to provide our employees with the knowledge and confidence to do the right thing and adopt more secure behaviours. We can do this by developing these moments that truly matter for all our people.

Note: *'Whaling for Beginners'* can be downloaded here:
https://www.axelos.com/resilia/whaling-for-beginners

4

CYBER SECURITY AND SMALL BUSINESSES

BALANCING RISK & REWARD

RICHARD KNOWLTON, RICHARD KNOWLTON ASSOCIATES LTD

Larger companies are beginning to get the message that effective cyber risk management is critical to their success.

Unfortunately, many SMEs[1] have yet to take action. That matters because their security vulnerabilities not only threaten their own operations but may also endanger other companies up and down their supply chain.

With everybody talking about the General Data Protection Regulation (GDPR)[2] and the latest hacking attack, those of you who run small businesses will have a lot of questions about cyber-security. However, it is not always easy to get answers that are relevant to your businesses. I have written this chapter with you in mind.

BUT WE'RE TOO SMALL TO HAVE TO CARE ABOUT CYBER-SECURITY

Look at the press almost any day, and there will be a report about the latest massive cyber-breach in a multinational corporation or even a government. Surely, the hackers only target the big players? Why would they come after a small business like mine?

---

1. The UK government and the EU have a shared definition of an SME: Micro Business = less than 10 employees & turnover under £2 million; Small Business = less than 50 employees & turnover under £10 million; Medium Business = Less than 250 employees & turnover under £50 million
2. See below.

Unfortunately, all the evidence shows that small businesses are as vulnerable as the multinationals. In March 2018, the Institute of Directors reported that 5.4 million small businesses in the UK had been attacked more than seven million times in a year[3].

Why is that? Because smaller companies are easier to hack. They often focus little on security and have fewer counter-measures in place. Meanwhile, smart criminals can use SMEs to hack into other companies in their supply chain.[4]

WHAT AN ATTACK COULD COST

You and your colleagues will have invested a great deal of time, emotion and hard cash in your business. You will be very keen to protect and grow that investment.

In developing your business strategy, you will already be looking at how you can manage a variety of business risks: how to compete with rival companies, manage your tax liability and comply efficiently with government regulation. That business strategy must also consider how you will minimise the chance of a cyber-incident and mitigate its consequences when it happens.

Why do you need to give cyber security this priority? A recent government report calculates £3,100 as the average cost of a cyber-attack leading to a loss of assets or data.[5] That does not sound a great deal, but just think about your wasted time, worry and the sheer nuisance involved. And remember the money you will have to spend to recover your IT systems and data after a successful cyber-attack.

At the same time, the incident will have a direct impact on your reputation with potential customers and suppliers, and so on the value of your business. Research shows that more than half of consumers are already uneasy about shopping with small companies online, and that over 80% of them would buy more if a business could show that it had good defences against cybercrime.

And finally, it may cost you a great deal of money in fines and legal fees too, because the government figure I quoted earlier takes no account of your legal responsibility to protect data privacy[6]. You must consult your legal advisers to understand your

---

3. See https://www.iod.com/ingoodcompany/article/7-shocking-facts-about-cyber-crime-and-uk-business. In early 2019, the government announced that 40% of all UK businesses had experienced a cyber-security breach or attack in the previous 12 months (Press release from Business Secretary Greg Clark, 28 January 2019).

4. In 2017, the US retail giant Target agreed to pay $18.5m to resolve litigation around a data breach which compromised the personal and credit card information of approximately 110 million Target customers. Cyber-criminals hacked Target's gateway server using credentials stolen from a third-party supplier, a refrigeration contractor.

5. See "Cyber Security Breaches Survey 2018" published by the Department of Digital, Culture, Media and Sport (DCMS), page 42 available at: https://assets.publishing.service.gov.uk/government/uploads/system/uploads/attachment_data/file/702074/Cyber_Security_Breaches_Survey_2018_-_Main_Report.pdf. The estimated total cost of breaches has consistently increased for medium businesses (specifically) since 2016.

6. The DCMS carried out its survey before the GDPR came into force in May 2018.

obligations under the General Data Protection Regulation (GDPR). Your company may be liable for severe penalties if it is non-compliant[7].

WHAT WE SHOULD BE WORRIED ABOUT EXACTLY

The following will give you a flavour, though this is a big subject. For most SMEs, the biggest threat is going to be from criminals trying to steal money[8].

The crooks will generally be looking to steal credit card or banking information, together with associated names, addresses and dates of birth. This means that they will target your staff records, together with your invoice, sales and customer payment databases.

Criminals will often try to extort money from you directly, too. In recent years, many companies have been victims of *ransomware* attacks where hackers smuggle *malware* on to your systems that encrypts and blocks access to your company data. They offer to decrypt the data on payment of a ransom, usually by way of an untraceable transfer of bitcoins.

Hackers are very smart about the amount of ransom they demand. It is usually just small enough to persuade you to pay up rather than face the hassle of going to the police. Unfortunately, though, just because you have paid does not necessarily mean that the hackers will keep their side of the deal. They have already moved on.

HOW CRIMINALS CARRY OUT THESE ATTACKS

In most cases, cyber-attacks start with emails[9], with hackers targeting people – us – to get through our defences.

The criminals will often use a technique known as *phishing*, where they send a message that appears to come from a source that you would instinctively trust: your bank, a government department, a supplier or even a friend.

The message may try to trick you into handing over sensitive information (usernames, passwords and credit card details). Or it may ask you to click on a link to view a document or fill out a form. When you do so, you will download some kind of malware designed to attack your company's IT network.

Another tried and tested criminal technique is to use an infected USB stick, perhaps left lying around in a carpark or outside your office. How many of us think twice before loading it into our computers? What's the harm in seeing what's on it…?

And finally, hackers can also get into your systems if you are running insecure WiFi

---

7. The Information Commissioner's Office (ICO) has the power to fine a non-compliant company up to £17m, or 4% of annual turnover, whichever is higher. Note that the UK government has committed to continued enforcement of GDPR after Brexit.
8. For some SMEs working in critical national infrastructure or industries like energy, the threat may come more from international state espionage. But the principles I describe in this article still apply.
9. They may also exploit other instant electronic message systems such as WhatsApp.

networks or are sharing a printer or scanner with another company with lax security controls.

WHAT I CAN DO TO PROTECT MY BUSINESS – TECHNOLOGY

I am going to argue later that your biggest security risk is probably not going to be with your technology. However, I certainly do **not** mean that the technical security of your IT systems is unimportant.

There is no such thing as perfect security, and certainly no silver bullet. But there is a lot you can do with IT to significantly reduce the risk of a successful attack and to control the fall-out if hackers do succeed in getting through your defences.

Remember that while there are lots of people out there trying to sell you expensive technical solutions (occasionally little more than snake oil remedies), a good defence does not need to cost you a lot of money. Most important of all, you should be as rigorous in your cost-benefit analysis of investments in security as you would be in taking any other business decision. That is what cyber security is all about - managing a business risk.

The chances are that you and your colleagues will not know much about IT security. So, I suggest the following steps[10].

First of all, identify the systems and databases that are really critical to your business. Every company is different, but no business wants to lose its financial data (for banking, invoicing and sales), or customer and supplier details. Think, too, about any valuable intellectual property you may have developed (that award-winning recipe, for example). And don't forget your staff records, for the reasons I mentioned earlier.

Next, check where this data is stored (on a server in your office or on the cloud?), and think about who has access to it: everybody, because that is the easiest way to work for a business your size, or only selected staff?

You then need to go into more detail. In particular, you need to understand:
Are we using up-to-date software? What upgrades are available[11]?

- A software upgrade will cost you money but think of it as a business – not just a security – investment. It may well also improve efficiency, reliability and the customer experience.
- What anti-virus programmes are we using? Do we keep them up-to-date?
- What devices (smartphones, tablets, PCs, laptops) have access to our systems? Do we issue staff with these devices, or do we allow them to use their own?

---

10. If you want to know more, there are plenty of good resources at hand. Start with the government's National Cyber Security Centre (NCSC) which was set up in 2017 to support UK business with cyber risk management. They have published a paper for SMEs at https://www.ncsc.gov.uk/guidance/cyber-security-small-business-guide-pdf-version. See also the FSB's paper at https://www.fsb.org.uk/docs/default-source/fsb-org-uk/FSB-Cyber-Resilience-report-2016.pdf?sfvrsn=0.
11. Remember that some manufacturers like Microsoft no longer support older versions of some standard programmes like Windows XP. As a result they longer issue updates and security patches for them. Check that you are not using any such "obsolete" software.

What measures do we have in place to ensure that these devices are as secure as possible?

— How often do we back up our critical databases and where are the backups held? This could be really important if your systems get locked in a ransomware attack.

— If we do not already have our own secure broadband or WiFi network, what would it cost to install? Remember once again that secure networks are an investment towards a well-run business, not just a cost.

— Are staff sending work emails and accessing our databases from outside the office, e.g. by using WiFi in Internet cafes, hotels and airports? Generally speaking, these WiFi systems are insecure. It could be that a simple Virtual Private Network (VPN) app could greatly improve your security at a small cost?[12]

— Could we reduce the number of people with access to our critical data while also retaining operational efficiency?

— How aware of the risks are those who do have such access?

When you have the answers, sit down with the people responsible for your IT network and talk through what you have found. You need a professional view of whether your arrangements are as good as they should be to manage the risks. You then need to understand what it will cost to raise your security to an acceptable level.

WHAT I CAN DO TO PROTECT MY BUSINESS – PEOPLE

All experience shows that hacking attacks rarely succeed because of a failure of technology.

In a small number of cases, one of your staff may deliberately compromise your security.[13] But usually hackers succeed because an employee has let them in, usually through carelessness or ignorance.

We all know that people can be careless, even when they know what is in their own interests. Despite intense public campaigns against drink-driving, smoking or unprotected sex, people still think that "it won't happen to me". And when it comes to their tablets, PCs or smartphones, many people put speed and convenience far ahead of thinking about security.

Obviously, if you and your staff have no idea what a phishing e-mail looks like, for example, that ignorance will greatly increase your company's vulnerability to a hacking attack. For this reason, many security managers talk about people being the "weakest

---

12. VPN enables users to send and receive data across shared or public networks as if their computing devices were directly connected to their private network. Applications running across the VPN can therefore benefit from the functionality, security, and management of your private network.

13. Sometimes employees ("insiders") are unhappy with a company, often because they have not received the recognition or the salary rise they think they deserve. Occasionally, they might think of taking it out on the company with a bit of sabotage. These "insiders" may be a particular threat because they will know exactly how your company works and how to mess with it if they are so inclined.

link" in cyber security. I like to turn this on its head. Your business's most important asset is your people and proper awareness training will turn them into your strongest defence against hackers.

GET YOUR STAFF ENGAGED

You need to ensure that two things happen to create a more cyber-secure environment for your business.

FIRST, EDUCATION
There are countless courses on the market, but I suggest that a mix of on-line teaching tools and interactive sessions with an external consultant is the best approach.

On-line tools are convenient, since staff can go through the teaching modules in their own time in the office. They take tests to show that they have understood the teaching material, with refresher training at regular intervals – perhaps every six or twelve months.

However, the drawback with on-line courses is that they may quickly become boring tick-box exercises to get through as quickly as possible. You need to combine them with motivational and engaging face-to-face teaching and discussion. That means bringing in a consultant.

What is this training going to cost? That will depend on how many staff you have to train, and the package that suits you best. Shop around, speak to your peers and consult your trade body, if you have one. Most important of all, you must not think of training as just an optional, non-priority cost. It should be a central part of your business strategy for protecting value in your company.

SECOND, SECURITY CULTURE
You need to create a culture in which secure behaviours are as much the norm as they are for health and safety. This will need a strong "tone from the top", because staff pick up very quickly when their bosses only pay lip-service to a company policy.

You could, for example, dedicate time in office meetings or at the coffee machine to discussing the latest hacking case in the news, or even among your staff, their friends and family. Sadly, you will not lack for material.

Get your people talking about whether it could have happened in your business, and what would have prevented it. Take every opportunity to remind your staff how serious you all need to be about managing cyber risk.

If you do this in the way that I have described, your staff will find it interesting and motivating – not least, of course, because what they learn is very relevant to their private lives and those of their families and friends.

Should you punish bad security behaviours? I do not personally see the value of "naming and shaming" people who make mistakes. It does not exactly give people a positive motivation, and it might make them less likely to own up if they slip up. Much better to publicly recognise and applaud people who consistently get things right.

BALANCING RISK AND REWARD

As I said earlier, you and your colleagues will be set on protecting and growing all the investment you are putting into expanding your business.

I cannot tell you what is most important for your business as you prioritise and control your costs. But do think very carefully indeed before you decide that an investment in your company's cyber-security is not a business priority.

Unless you act now, a cyber-attack could seriously undermine everything you have worked to achieve. Always remember that you **will** suffer a hacking attack - or may already have done so, even if you don't know it!

5

THERE IS NO SUCH THING AS A FREE LUNCH

HOW CRIMINALS USE OUR GREED AGAINST US

NICK IOANNOU, BOOLEAN LOGICAL LTD

Today's online world is awash with marketing offers for free services, discount vouchers and free trials for annual subscriptions. We have got so used to the 'free for end users' business model, as used by the likes of Facebook, Google, and so many others, we now regularly do not expect to pay for so many things online. This coupled with society's need for instant gratification and the ease of digital piracy and theft, has made the internet a criminal's paradise.

Part of the problem is that people don't see online theft as theft, because it is a digital copy. The original is still there, therefore nothing has been stolen as such, compared to the real world. This makes it easier for people to happily download pirated movies, music and software as they don't feel like a shoplifter for doing so. As far as they are concerned, they never had the money to buy the product anyway, so the company never lost a potential sale. Illegal streaming services also add to the mix, to watch movies and live events, which is considered less of a problem by many people because there is nothing stored on your devices afterwards.

Another part of the problem is our whole culture of grabbing a bargain, the whole psychology of sales and how it makes people act. People have physically fought over stuff just because it is half price in department stores. They have literally risked imprisonment for a piece of clothing or a television set. So, when presented with an online bargain for a product or subscription service, people generally do not stop to think and ask if this is too good to be true. Greed is a major factor behind much of this, as we are constantly told we need the latest, fastest, smallest, just released, of everything and anything. Much of this is out of most people's reach financially, so the offers of something for free or vastly reduced make excellent bait for the criminals.

We also have the freemium business model where basic functions are free, but premium features are chargeable. Often this also includes free trials of the premium features. This is the model used by Spotify, LinkedIn and hundreds of others, but can be easily abused where contract commitments for the premium features are unclear or the terms and conditions of the free service gives an unreasonable amount of access and invasion of privacy.

So, let's be clear, it's not just criminals we need to be wary of. There are a lot of dubious and grey areas that some businesses use to prey on unwitting customers, adding unnecessary charges or hidden fees. Also, let's not forget the genuine businesses, where the real cost (not necessarily in money terms) is buried in their terms and conditions, of which people are often not made aware. This is now against data protection law and as a result more and more firms are being fined. Here's a list of what you might encounter online:

Outright fake and illegal
Fake official websites
Fake online store
Fake discount vouchers
Fake gift cards or vouchers
Fake digital subscription
Fake streaming service
Fake digital in-game currency
Fake crypto-currencies
Fake software
Fake online service
Fake online casino credits
Fake loans
Fake competitions
Software keygen utilities

Grey and dubious
Unofficial websites with unnecessary fees
Online stores with fake reviews
Overpriced subscription services after free trial
Overpriced competitions and quizzes made to look like part of a website

Genuine businesses
You supply personal information
You give up image rights to your photos
You supply location data and activity information
You supply spending patterns and preferences
Reverse auction platforms

Let's start with outright fake and illegal side of things. Many of these rely on email, social media messaging, SMS text messages, typosquatting and dubious adverts to get you to visit their webpages. Some will pay to be on the first page of the major search engines, but generally this is not the case. More and more criminals are targeting smartphone users as the smaller screen and quirks of the web browser aids them in carrying out their deception. The fact that the full web address is hidden and that mobile versions of websites look different anyway, makes it so much easier to convince you that nothing is amiss.

Receiving a targeted message asking you to renew a license or permit that points to a fake version of an official website can be very problematic. In the UK, many people have been duped into buying a fake annual road tax for their car or a fake TV license. They still owe the money for the official documents but can now be fined for not having them. Also, there is the problem that they have paid money to the criminals, who now have their payment details and home addresses. As many official websites encourage direct debit as the preferred form of payment, often with some minor discount, if the criminals offer this too, then they will also have your bank details if you fall for the scam, leading to possible identity fraud. In the UK, Her Majesty's Revenue and Customs (HMRC) is one of the most targeted of the government's websites, because the criminals know everyone has to pay taxes. Fake tax refund email scams are so common that HMRC's security division took down over 20,000 malicious web domains in 2018.

Fake online stores pose a similar problem as you get tricked into giving your payment details, name, address and contact info. Price is the main lure here; typically high value electronics either supposedly coming from a reputable supplier or some other reason like liquidated stock or cancelled orders. Time pressures can be added like "only 2 left in stock" and "9 people are also looking at this item" to try and get you to make a quick decision. Store reviews can also easily be faked or bought by the criminals, to try and help build the illusion of reputation and legitimacy.

There are a lot of people who use online discount vouchers from the many free reputable websites like Groupon, Wowcher, Vouchercodes, RetailMeNot, etc. Unfortunately, there are also a lot of fake vouchers online too, trying to trick you into visiting malicious websites to phish you for your account credentials, payment information and or glean lots of personal information. Vouchers that are gift cards worth a nominal amount of money in a particular store are increasingly issued as digital codes via email. This makes them extremely attractive to criminals both as something to steal and sell on, or to fake. But it is not just online and traditional retailers that are being targeted. Social media and many online gaming platforms offer some type of digital currency or online wallets, which gives the criminals a wide range of opportunities to offer this as bait: typically, as free digital currency or massively discounted purchase options.

When it comes to digital currencies though, the cryptocurrencies are a criminal's dream. They have become the new way to rob banks, except now the banks are the cryptocurrency exchanges. Many people have jumped on the bandwagon and invested in cryptocurrencies like Bitcoin, which has turned some who invested in the early years into millionaires. But unlike stocks and shares, you could also invest in the technology and 'create' or earn the cryptocurrencies typically known as mining. Quickly the criminals realised there was an opportunity to get others to do this for them without them being aware, infecting machines that would mine for them overnight. In fact they also realised that they could persuade people that they could earn from the whole venture, while secretly knowing that they have everything they needed to steal from them at a later date. It's a bit like meeting some random person in the street who tells you about an investment opportunity, and you go and open a bank account with them at a bank you've never heard of.

Our online world is paid for typically by either someone else in the form adverts, or us directly as a subscription. So, once again the criminals try to convince us that they can offer us something for a fraction of the cost. I've even seen emails trying to convince people to pay for a messaging service that is now completely free. You couldn't pay for it, even if you wanted too. Some of the most popular online subscriptions are for streaming services, for films, TV and music, like Netflix, Spotify and this makes it easy for them to offer attractive too good to be true deals. Also beware of anyone claiming to give you access to premium streaming content for free, as often the 'video codec' required to watch it which needs to be installed first, may also do other more malicious things.

Over the years many people have been tricked into installing malware because they wanted a software package that they couldn't afford or didn't want to pay for. Commercial software can cost thousands, so for some people they'd rather find an illegal copy or download a piece of software that would generate the necessary license codes to activate a trial version. These key generator utilities often have ulterior motives, containing malware and remote access trojans. One of the most copied pieces of software over the years has been Adobe Photoshop which for many years cost over £600 to buy and version updates were over £200 each. Today though, it is available as an official subscription together with Adobe Lightroom for just £9.98 a month with version updates included, yet people are still risking their security to illegally download a 'free' version.

While it is a lot easier to be wary of the fake and illegal, the grey and dubious online world is a lot harder to see coming. Here online businesses (if you can call them that) have pushed the boundaries of the law, all for the sake of profit. Through clever search engine techniques, these businesses can place themselves higher in the rankings than official government websites to pay for things like road tolls, driving licences and road tax. In the UK, the DVLA receives reports of thousands of suspected scams and misleading hidden fees.

Another way they can make money is to trick you into calling premium rate phone numbers which route through to the official low-cost number, pocketing the difference. To give you an idea of the scale of the problem, again HRMC in the UK had over 5M redirects from recovered domains using premium rate numbers. The scams evolved to the point where the criminals have been spoofing the official HMRC phone number for text messages and now even leaving automated voicemail messages with the (premium rate) number to call.

Unnecessary fees are another trick where a fake official website charges for something that does not have a fee or charges a higher fee than the official one, before passing on the information to be processed by the genuine website. If they fail to pass on the information though due to technical issues, you could yourself facing penalty fines as well. Staying with the theme of overcharging, a lucrative market is the abuse of the subscription after a free trial business model. Here overpriced subscriptions or recurring plans are often aimed at smartphone users, who don't realise that the service or use of the app will incur such a high monthly or weekly charge. Here the 'businesses' are relying on you forgetting to cancel and then using the 30-day cancellation period terms to milk more money out of you once you realise what has happened.

Other tricks include asking to authorise a recurring payment to 'unlock' premium features in an app that would normally only cost you only £2.99 as a one-off payment, but instead you find yourself being billed this monthly. To give you an idea of just how lucrative this can be, one QR Code Reader in the Apple App Store earned the company behind it over $5 million via their nasty $156 a year subscription.

Tricking people is a lot easier on a smartphone due to a number of reasons. The screen is much smaller than a laptop or tablet, together with mobile versions of websites which hide certain information that is easy to see on a computer web browser. These ease of use interface changes allow things like the true web address to be hidden or important terms and conditions to be pushed to the very bottom of a long webpage. One of the dubious practices I have had to deal with is overpriced competitions and quizzes that were made to look like part of a website, when they were in fact adverts that had nothing to do with the website owner. Worst still the website concerned ran a weekly competition and the advert was styled to look like one of the questions, when in fact it took you to a completely different website that charged £6 a question. The alert to say that there would be charge is easily missed on a small screen and to make matters worse, mobile payments are charged directly to your network provider and do not need any form of confirmation. So, in a matter of minutes, a colleague was tricked into answering five questions and instantly billed £30 for the privilege.

Another dubious practice we face are the online stores with fake reviews for their products and services. Items that only have five-star reviews in a very short space of time are highly suspicious, especially if there are a lot of them. These can be quite easy to spot in say a 400-page book, that all the reviewers left within a day of the purchase. People sell review services on freelancing websites, as well as mass Twitter and Instagram followers to boost the status and appearance on those platforms. Sticking to mainstream online stores with a trusted returns policy can help, as you know you will get a refund if you are not satisfied.

Finally, we get the genuine businesses that hide the 'true' none monetary cost of using their services. These are the businesses that buried in their terms and conditions, sell on your information to interested parties. With every free online service you use, it is important to identify how they can afford to make it free? Online infrastructure is not cheap if you have to support tens of thousands of users. Common methods are to offer paid for premium services, run adverts alongside, treat the whole thing as a brand awareness exercise, sell the data they collect on you, or a mixture.

Other things that a business or organisation can sell on is the image usage rights to any of your photos that you post on their online platforms. Many of the popular social media platforms include in their terms and conditions the ability for them to use anything you post and also that it is transferable or sub-licensable.

Profiling of users has been become an art form that is so granular with over 5000 unique aspects that can be recorded about a person. Spending an advertising budget on heavily targeted people yields high returns, which is why these companies go to great lengths to infer and establish your spending patterns and current life stage or personal situation. Everything you do online within a particular website or service may be tracked and go towards building a profile of you, which is often sold on.

Adverts for reverse auction platforms sound too good to be true but are in fact genuine. What they don't tell you in the advert is that there is a fee to place a bid. It doesn't matter if the item, say an Apple iPhone sells for £9.29, what matters is the number of bid entries required before the auction closes. So, if it costs £5 to bid, and 250 bids are required, the auction website collects £1,250 plus the lowest unique bid. Assuming that is, that the auction platform is playing by the rules.

There many more things to look out for between the criminals, the grey and dubious, and legitimate businesses, but hopefully you now have a good understanding of what goes on online and who is paying for what, because as the saying goes, "there is no such thing as a free lunch." Someone, somewhere has to pay up; just make sure your desire to get something at a bargain is not letting you get tricked into paying, in more ways than you expect.

Cybersecurity

What have you got to lose?

Cybersecurity is one of the most challenging issues facing businesses. In today's interconnected world, all companies and their customers are potential targets for cyberattacks.

DLA Piper's global cybersecurity team are well positioned to assist clients in managing this risk area. We can quickly and cost effectively assist you to navigate an emergency cyber incident or to implement a 360-degree approach to creating, managing and maintaining a secure cyber-DNA.

For more information please contact: **cybersecurity@dlapiper.com**

DLA PIPER

Beecher Madden

We are a leading UK and US cyber security recruitment business. Leveraging our long-held relationships, industry knowledge and data driven approach, we help candidates and clients make better hiring decisions.

www.beechermadden.com

⟨ RESILIA° FRONTLINE

EFFECTIVE CYBER SECURITY AWARENESS TRAINING FOR ALL YOUR EMPLOYEES

Ensuring your most **valuable and precious information** remains secure from cyber-attacks is now a critical priority for every organization. But your cyber security is only as good as the attitudes and behaviours of *your people*.

RESILIA® Frontline, our **GCHQ Certified Cyber Training**, gives your employees, the **simple, practical guidance** they need to make the right decisions at the right time.

- Short, engaging, relevant and regular online cyber security and data protection awareness training available in multiple languages

- 12 subject areas across five learning pathways: Managing Online Risk, Keeping Safe Online, Protecting Information, Safe Device Use and Data Protection and the GDPR

- Written and designed by international cyber security and learning and development specialists

- Awareness content available in multiple formats - games, animations and videos, eLearning and tests, diagnostics, audio stories and pdfs to suit different learning preferences

- Ability to create your own tailored awareness campaigns to suit your specific cyber risks and vulnerabilities

- Measure, learn and adapt via a comprehensive management information suite.

Make your people your greatest defence against cyber-attacks today!

Visit AXELOS.com/resilia-frontline to find out more and request a live demonstration of RESILIA Frontline.

FOR MORE INFORMATION ON HOW TO MANAGE CYBERSECURITY RISK, TAKE A LOOK AT THE TWO PREVIOUS EDITIONS.

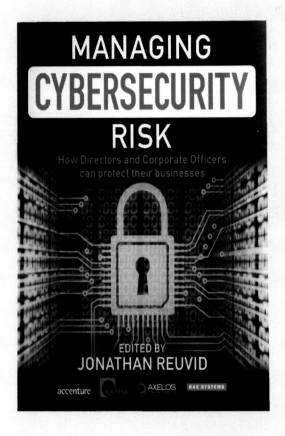

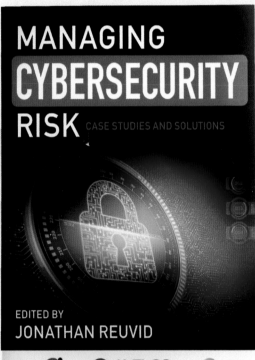

MANAGING CYBERSECURITY
RISK 2016

How Directors and Corporate Officers
can protect their businesses

Published: November 30, 2016
ISBN (Paperback): 9781785079153
ISBN (Ebook): 9781785079146

MANAGING CYBERSECURITY
RISK 2017

Case Studies and Solutions

Published: October 31, 2017
ISBN (Paperback): 9781787198913
ISBN (Ebook): 9781787198906

PART TWO

ADDRESSING THE THREATS
TO YOUR BUSINESS

6

INSIDER OUT

WHY SECURING YOUR BUSINESS FROM INSIDER THREATS IS CRITICAL FOR DATA SECURITY

CHRIS GREANY, TEMPLAR EXECUTIVES LTD

In any security regime, a layered approach is generally accepted as the best way forward. Approaching risk and threat in an incremental and proportionate way ensures that your company can flourish while keeping what is important to your business safe.

THE NATURE OF INSIDER THREATS

For me, insiders fall into three main buckets: the foolish, the lazy and the criminal. The foolish is all of us. If we are not aware of the risk and have not been trained, we make innocent mistakes. The lazy are those that go around company policies designed to protect information and keep it secure. Often they are not bad actors; sometimes the company makes security so difficult and the policy too complex that to do a good job employees are unwittingly forced to breach them. That is no good for anyone. Sharing lap top devices with a single password is just one example of poor information security, but what if the company doesn't supply everyone with a lap top? Finally, the criminal; they may have joined the company for that sole reason, a bad actor, but they may have changed over time and gone bad? Did they miss a promotion? Are they not being listened to? A toxic work culture maybe? Perhaps they are going through a traumatic life event. I don't seek to justify it, but people "go rogue" for many reasons and the signs are often there, if you are looking. They could have once been the lazy insider everyone kept talking about, but did nothing to alert or find out what was wrong. The point I make is that the signs are there if people know how to look.

It is strange therefore that insider risk is still seen by many as not as important as, for instance, perimeter protection, the place where the techies live; "*the real cyber defences*" as someone once said to me. If you consider the fort and walls principle, you can have the best defensive walls, the best bricks and the best builders, but if your threat actor has legitimate access to the fort already you are just throwing good money away. Insider language also can be confusing. As highlighted earlier, insider risk isn't just about the malicious people, although some of the greatest data breaches in history have happened because of this. Edward Snowden for instance. It is also about employees just trying to do their job well but because they haven't been made aware of risks, such as sending data outside or clicking links, they unwittingly expose the organisation to business risk. Cyber security is not just about techies and coders it's also about people, psychology and understanding human behaviour.

THE CHALLENGES OF NEW HIRES

Even trying to stop a malicious insider joining is a challenge. Many companies still separate the human from the tech from the security. Humans sit with Human Resources and from the very start, the moment they apply or are recruited for work, the system falls down if all those entities are not at least talking to each other.

Standing up any insider risk program has to be a holistic framework bringing together the different entities in your organisation.

As organisations' understanding matures, the Chief Security Officer more often owns some of the Cyber and Information Security risk as well, often jointly with the CIO. The CISOs will also sometimes report to these people. But the insider risk, which is also an information security risk, still seems to get bounced between HR and many other places. It is still in many companies a little homeless, and ready to be easily exploited by bad actors.

Screening is a perennial question and in the heavily regulated sectors, particular finance, additional annual re-screening for regulated persons is mandatory. But screening is a point in time only, nothing more; it is no deeper than a search of pre-defined indices, usually criminal, credit and bankruptcy. Even when prospective people fail this stage, the hiring manager is consulted and sometimes the prospective hire still joins the company. There may be good and fair reasons for this, but if the conversation does not include the security team, then much of the pieces of the puzzle are missing. The hiring manager wants the hire, which also creates a conflict especially if they get a bounty for it. Pre-employment screening is certainly an HR function, but the risk when it goes wrong is a business risk problem, a security problem, and a company reputational problem. Then there is integrity of the data; some countries still have paper based criminal justice systems. There has to be input, consultancy and veto allowed if the security team judge that the risk is unacceptable. I haven't yet mentioned the word cyber in this paragraph, but once that person is in and on your network, you have given them some keys to your fort. The perimeter has been breached, and no amount of external monitoring will have seen it.

And now they are in, how were they on-boarded? Given a laptop and login as a welcome? As they are new, the first week is spent meeting new people and surfing the intranet looking at things on the company system, being curious. And that's how it should be, right? But how long was spent explaining to them the acceptable use policy and the sanctions behind it? Most likely it's buried in their contract. And now the working environment is one of hot desk. Different lost souls passing through each day, no one knows each other, and a new person looks no different to all the other people wandering about looking for a perch. From the intern to the longstanding staffer, they are indistinguishable. Traditional supervisor checks and balances no longer exist, and your new manager might not even be in your workspace, or even in the same country.

There is a better way. When the job offer arrives, this is the time to begin engagement, a simple welcome video sent to the new worker, starting the info-sec security journey before they arrive? They will feel that your company is already investing in them. Alternatively, they could just tick "I agree" at the end of that twenty-page contract, where page one was the salary and acceptable use was page eighteen. Legally all is good, the compliance boxes have been ticked, but security wise?

One of the other biggest concerns is the number of people who have user access privileges; it's remarkable how little attention is paid to this when in essence another set of keys this time allows the user or a bad actor deeper into the organisation where password and credentials may be hiding in plain sight. Monitoring and logging "*per se*", whether it is for privilege access, printing, email or web use, serves a useful audit function; like CCTV you can go back and see what happened, but if it is not live monitored like CCTV the event has happened, and with data leaving, it is gone. And if the data logging sources aren't good then false positives just create further work for those techies and with it more spend.

Many organisations also report that one of the barriers to successfully addressing both the malicious and non-malicious insider risk is the lack of collaboration between departments in companies. Cultural barriers, working in silos and inter-departmental rivalry all combine to allow insiders to be successful; this in itself is an insider risk and company culture at strategic level heavily influences this either negatively or positively.

Although the ability to detect and monitor now is an excellent step forward, everyone knows prevention is key. It's better long term. Just as in policing, arresting people all day may look like good activity, but reducing criminality would be far better and cheaper long term.

The move into different ways of identifying possible insider activity early is the sweet spot to aim for, and if you are running a SOC it's the natural home, together with any existing cyber response. Employee behaviour monitoring is still a conversation had in whispers and it brings with it the question of privacy, ethics and legitimacy, which have to be carefully considered. It also adds to the debate of what should employees be allowed to do on the company's time on the company network, which comes back to the acceptable use policy. You know the one, buried in the contract, page eighteen that no one has explained to you yet.

And once the employee begins, from day one, continuous awareness and training is the first and most important step in preventing a whole host of insider threats. Phishing for instance is still the number one cyber attack vector; even with the best perimeter, phishing emails still reach the end user. Whether the employee is a junior trainee or a member of the board, all need to have some form of awareness training. Indeed, board members and people of significance need more training I would argue, especially around Spear Phishing. This includes the PA's and Admins who often access their Principals' accounts. And if you are now wondering what is the difference between phishing and spear phishing it is worth looking up. Phishing simulations are also one of the best ways to measure if employee security culture is improving; evidence shows that they have a positive effect in reducing click rates. The next step is what to do that with that suspect phish; deleting it is good, but you will never know if it was a phish or not. Employees are curious, they need feedback so there should be a place for them to highlight the phish and have it safely inspected. There needs to be feedback. There is nothing better for an employee than to get a thank you for keeping the company safe; they feel better about the company and will think more about protecting it.

Still, in many places this never happens; people muddle along, pressing buttons, clicking links, winning "prizes" and then lock out, ransomware, malware or worse. It's too late then, you have been breached. But that perimeter security still looks really good though, from the outside. There is also the human problem of ego: "I'm too important for this as I am very senior…" Organisations need to set standards and culture from the top with an aspiration of zero exception, without personal emotion. Longer-term the company is safer, the regulatory authorities are happier as are your clients. No one individual can be bigger than the company.

BEST PRACTICE

Whether you have 100,000 employees or 50, organisations should think about the most appropriate solution to reduce the insider risk. Small companies, especially when it comes to business email compromise, phishing and procurement fraud are particularly vulnerable, and just one successful attack could shut down the business. It doesn't need to be this way with appropriate, often low cost measures.

Trends are changing also in terms of data commoditisation, and threat vector. While financial data such as credit cards are widely for sale on the dark web, more and more breaches are reported around health data. Experian recently published the dark web prices for cards at $1-100 and health records at $1-1000. Deloitte recently assessed the Health Care Industry spending to be $10+ Trillion by 2020.

In terms of InfoSec maturity, health care is still at the very beginning, and recent trends indicate that the health sector is becoming the rolling target for cyber attacks and criminality. And health care is linked to insurance markets and the rolling supply chain it uses. The Wannacry attack that affected the UK's NHS in 2017 was a wake up call, and with the support of the UK's National Cyber Security Centre and NHS Digital, progress is being made in transforming cyber security culture and understanding in the NHS. The risk to healthcare is also a patient risk. Across the world, patient's lives depend on data having integrity, being available and for all the networked devices to be safe. A ransomware lock out on a CT scanner has life changing consequences. It only takes one human to click on a link, or to act maliciously. For some organisations it will mean data loss, for others shut down. In health it's all of those as well as lives.

Now I may have painted in some areas a depressingly familiar picture, which often sounds like the conversations being had around cyber security from ten years ago. The good news is that more and more companies and organisations are having the conversation about insider risk. Some are also seeing this as an information risk and security driven function bringing all areas together under an enterprise security framework, which is a demonstration of company maturity and recognition that silos are a barrier to safety. The perimeter security is critical but so is the culture and people. As organisations get better and procure more and more tech, the criminals will seek to exploit more and more the human element. Every human is different; that is why Insider and Cyber is one and the same thing. It's not just a tech thing; it's a human thing, a people thing.

7

INSIDE THREAT

BALANCING GOOD INFORMATION SECURITY PRACTICES WITH DATA PROTECTION AND EMPLOYMENT

ROSS MCKEAN, SAM MILLAR, CHRISTIAN SCHOOP, ARMIN HENDRICH, JAN POHLE, JAN SPITTKA, KATHERINE GIBSON AND MARIUS HAAK, DLA PIPER

Insider threat comes in many forms and is a factor common to many data and security incidents. Human error such as errant emails, errant uploads to publicly available resources or lost laptops and flash drives are a perennial challenge for organisations. Malicious attacks also often involve insiders though detection is challenging; it is difficult to single out bad behaviour from normal business as usual activities, particularly when the rogue staff member has privileged access rights. Other common examples of insider threats include third parties authorised to access corporate networks. Security is only as good as the weakest link in the chain and several high profile data breaches have demonstrated that the weakest link is frequently in the supply chain. Another common cause of insider related incidents is terminated staff who take data with them to their next employer or who retain access rights – often caused by lax policing and termination of access controls when staff leave.

Data breaches and security incidents arising from insider threat can cause very serious harm to an organisation including loss of valuable intellectual property, reputational damage and loss of trust and – where personal data are involved – the risk of revenue based fines and potentially ruinous group claims for compensation.

The on-going litigation in the UK between Wm Morrison Supermarkets and a group of just under 6,000 staff illustrates the potential exposure[1]. The Court of Appeal held that Wm Morrison Supermarkets plc was vicariously liable for the criminal actions of an employee (Mr Skelton) who had maliciously, and with the intention of damaging

---

1. Wm Morrison Supermarkets Plc v Various Claimants [2018] EWCA Civ 2339

Morrisons' reputation, misused the personal data of nearly 100,000 Morrisons' employees. This decision was reached despite Morrisons not being blamed by the court for the way that it handled its employees' personal data, and the fact that Mr Skelton's actions were an act of vengeance against the company. Morrisons was held to be liable for the data breach, leaving it open to a potentially vast compensation bill. Morrisons has appealed to the Supreme Court.

The Morrisons judgement has compounded the risk of insider threat for organisations by in effect concluding that even where an organisation has met its legal obligations to keep personal data safe and secure, it can nevertheless be held to be vicariously liable for the criminal wrongdoing of a rogue member of staff. However, this does not apply to all legal systems and all areas of law. In the German administrative sanctions law for example, liability for an employer is excluded if the competent managers comply with their supervisory duties.

So what should organisations do to mitigate the risk of insider threat?

PREVENTION IS BETTER THAN CURE

As with many enterprise risks, the solution is a combination of good policy, training and technology. However insider threat also creates a unique conundrum for organisations. While on the one hand a core requirement of the General Data Protection Regulation[2] ("GDPR") is to ensure that personal data are kept secure and not exposed to unauthorised disclosure or access[3], on the other hand many of the controls organisations implement to detect and prevent insider threat involve potentially highly invasive processing of staff personal data which may itself create liability under GDPR and similar data protection and, for many European jurisdictions, labour laws. Care therefore needs to be taken when designing and operating controls to tackle insider threat.

Having in place rigorous and thorough data protection policies and controls, as required under the GDPR regime, should diminish the risk to organisations; despite the fact that, in the unique circumstances of the Morrisons case, more stringent controls probably would not have prevented the breach or the court's finding.

Nevertheless, there are several key steps every organisation should take as part of its GDPR and general risk management regime in an effort to mitigate insider threat in the UK and Germany, including:

1. **Establish a cyber risk management policy and ensure that this is part of the company's governance framework.** This should address not only external risks, but internal risks posed by employees and workers. It should include provision for review and analysis to ensure that the policy can evolve with evolving risk and threats.

---

2. 679/2016/EU
3. Article 32 GDPR

2. **Review and update any existing IT Security policy or Acceptable Use of IT policy.** These should set standards of behaviour and advise employees that action can be taken if they breach the same. The policy should make it clear that employee emails and communications may be reviewed in the case of suspicion and that monitoring may take place to ensure compliance with policy (see point 6 below).

3. **Adequate training and user awareness.** Every organisation has a "weak spot" in its own staff. An adequate cyber security system should not only have the relevant defences and policies in place described above, but staff should be adequately trained on all relevant policies and procedures.

4. **Ensure internet safety and network security.** Networks should be protected against internal attacks, as well as external ones. There are basic security controls that can be implemented, even before more sophisticated tools are put in place. For example, by controlling access to removable media (such as memory sticks) and scanning all media before incorporating them into network systems. This should include an assessment of access controls and Administrator/Super-User status to ensure that access to the company's most sensitive data is limited to only those who need to have access to the same for their roles. Access rights should also be regularly reviewed to ensure that staff access is justified. Leaver procedures should ensure that staff access to systems is immediately terminated on their termination of employment and that laptops and other devices are returned. Similarly when IT devices are upgraded, controls should be in place to ensure that all devices are securely wiped of company data. This can be particularly challenging for devices using solid state drive technology.

5. **Review recruitment practices.** Many employers no longer ask for references, but these should be secured to verify employment history. In roles where employees pose particular risks to the business, it is possible to consider adopting background checking and vetting including in some cases criminal background checks. In the UK, this will usually be permitted, provided that the checks themselves and the means of carrying out them out are proportionate to meet a clear business need. For example, in the UK, it may be possible to carry out credit checks on employees with access to financial information or where a specific risk is identified – depending always on the level of such risk and the other controls in place. However, the rules for vetting, particularly where criminal background checks are undertaken, vary quite significantly from country to country so employees should seek legal advice. A data privacy impact assessment ("DPIA") should be carried out and carefully documented, along with the employer's proposed safeguards to ensure that vetting controls are managed carefully in practice.

6. **Consider network monitoring.** There are a number of monitoring tools available to employers. These include CCTV and email reviews, but also more sophisticated technologies such as Document Loss Prevention software, network immune tools and AI-lead software designed to learn user's "normal" behaviours and detect suspected bad behaviours. As with vetting (point 5 above) the monitoring system will need to be carefully designed to be proportionate to meet the company's needs and the relevant risks to ensure compliance with GDPR, data protection and labour laws. A DPIA will be needed to ensure that it does not present a high risk to employees. Further, employees should be fully advised of what types of monitoring activity are taking place in the workplace. This should include (a) the purpose for the activity; (b) the circumstances in which it may take place; (c) the nature of the monitoring or background checking; (d) how information obtained through the activity will be used; and (e) the safeguards in place for the employees who are subject to the activity. Certain measures may be subject to works council approval where a works council has been established.

7. **Consider risks posed by particular employees and consider how to manage these.** It may be that an employer has an aggrieved IT or finance team or unhappy senior manager. These grievances and issues should not be left to fester, but instead should be addressed effectively so that they do not morph into security risks. Similarly, employees with possible financial issues should be supported (as far as possible) so that they do not become targets for blackmail or bribes. To this end, it may be possible to carry out intermittent credit checks on key staff where this can be justified on the basis of the risk to the organisation. As with recruitment vetting, this will require a DPIA and careful consideration before implementation.

PRACTICE MAKES PERFECT

Security incidents arising from insider threat do pose some unique challenges given the potential for one or more "bad actors" to be within the compromised organisation. However, as with any enterprise risk, mitigation starts with a good incident response policy, the right governance and staff to implement that policy, and regular training in the form of table top exercises.

The crisis response team (internal and external) should comprise all the skill sets required for effective incident response including in particular cyber security forensics; communications and legal. Data breach is now a business as usual risk which happens at a low level on a daily basis for many larger organisations. Good policy and regular rehearsals will help organisations to "normalise" incident response and mitigate the risk of a data breach developing into a corporate crisis.

INSURANCE?

Insurance has a role to play but is not a silver bullet. In the Morrisons case, the court observed that the best way to guard against the risks posed by potential rogue employees is for employers to insure not only against corporate system failures and negligence by individuals acting in the course of their employment, but also against losses caused by dishonest or malicious employees. Cyber insurance is now essential for businesses that control and process data given the more stringent data protection regime imposed by the GDPR. However, malicious conduct, such as Mr Skelton's, may fall outside the scope of a standard cyber insurance policy. In addition, most policies also do not cover the prospect of fines that are issued by the regulators for breaches of the GDPR. As a result, it would be advisable not to rely on insurance provision, but instead to consider what steps can be taken to prevent this type of activity from occurring in the first place.

IF THE WORST HAPPENS

If a security incident occurs, the organisation will need to respond appropriately to this. Whilst a full discussion of breach response best practice is outside of the scope of this chapter, some particular challenges where insiders are involved in the UK and Germany are set out below.

INSIDERS AND THE INVESTIGATION
It is good practice to design policies and run investigations bearing in mind that bad actors might be on the inside of the organisation. If an insider is suspected, care should be taken to ensure that he/she is not party to the investigation and that they have no access to the investigation team's communications. Of course, it may not be apparent at the early stages of an investigation whether an insider is involved so the prudent approach is to design policies and investigate on the basis that they may be. Investigating teams should be kept to a minimum size and information shared (other than through controlled communications) on a strict need to know basis. For some organisations with a particular vulnerability to insider threat, it may make sense to invest in a separate confidential IT infrastructure so that investigations can be run "off-net" to maximise security and minimise the risk of tipping off bad actors with access to the organisation's IT infrastructure. In the case of unlawfuly obtained business secrets by a (new) employee, it is recommended to separate the data from the daily work and not to use it in order to avoid sanctions and damage claims against the company.

DOCUMENTS AND EVIDENCE
Log files which are often crucial to investigations are particularly important evidence when an insider is involved in the incident and they should be preserved as soon as possible. Care also needs to be taken not to "tread on the evidence" given that log files

and other evidence may be required to prove particular facts to regulators or in court and mishandling log file evidence may compromise their evidentiary value. Effective incident response therefore requires good forensic practices.

Any individuals required to produce documents should be informed about the purpose, scope and importance of the investigation. This will enable them to identify relevant documents and treat the investigation with the seriousness it merits. It is important to treat all relevant employees equally, as any sign of favouritism or discrimination could affect the way the results of the investigation are viewed.

This said, the investigation will often require the employer to undertake actions which employees may not immediately be aware of – such as reviewing email accounts, system logs or reviewing an individual's behaviour prior to the event taking place. This is likely to be possible in the UK, although the company will need to tread carefully to ensure that this behaviour is lawful. In particular, the company will need to carry out an assessment of the privacy risk to the individual against the business need to investigate. This balancing test will usually come down on the side of the company, provided that there is a genuine suspicion, employees are aware that emails may be accessed or monitored (see point 2 above) and the organisation will carry out a targeted, direct, search only for relevant material. In addition, it is possible to review emails marked personal in the UK if the company is able to justify this on balance. However, the company is not permitted to undertake a "fishing expedition" or review obviously irrelevant emails or data; even in cases of serious breaches.

INTERNATIONAL TRANSFERS

It is worth noting that care needs to be taken in investigations which span borders, as the justification for searching employee emails or accessing logs inside of Europe may not extend to countries which do not offer the same level of data protection as the UK, Germany or elsewhere in Europe. Any data that is transferred or accessed outside of Europe should be strictly limited to what is in fact necessary for a specific purpose (such as litigation or disciplinary action). What can be transferred is unlikely to be whole folders or email accounts, as only relevant documents are likely to be needed to be shared. Again, there are various balancing and risk assessments that need to be carried out in support of this exercise and documentation is required, including the implementation of adequate safeguards (if these are not already in place or a relevant exemption does not apply).

WITNESSES

As suggested above, the initial investigation should focus on fact-finding in order to allow the company to understand the breach, its effects (particularly on any individuals) and how to remediate the same. For this reason, if an insider is suspected, the company will wish to avoid tipping him/her off and securing their participation in the investigation process. As a result, companies may find that they need to cast the net wide when interviewing potential witnesses and taking action to secure evidence to avoid inadvertently highlighting who it is that is suspected.

If the perpetrator's identity is unknown, suspects should be interviewed as soon as possible. Until it is established who is involved, a cautious approach should be adopted. From the company's point of view, it is safer to withdraw authority and deny access to a larger number of people. However, this will have to be balanced against the risk of souring relations with innocent staff. If the individual is known, the risk posed by the individual during the investigation stage should be carefully reviewed and suspension from the network and from their employment should considered as an option to protect the business during the process. However, bear in mind that a suspended employee is out of the office and you will have no control or visibility of his/her actions and therefore you may need to consider how best to manage this in practice.

In Germany, if the Public Prosecutor's Office ("PPO") should be involved it is crucial not to interview suspected persons; otherwise the PPO will not undertake any secret investigation measures against the suspected persons (such as search and seizures). Therefore, when filing a criminal complaint it should be discussed with the PPO if and when an interview with the suspected persons or witnesses should take place.

DISCIPLINARY ACTION

Notwithstanding the above, once the data breach has been fully investigated and the company's suspicions confirmed, the company can move to take disciplinary action against the individual concerned. The investigation described above can form the basis of any disciplinary action, meaning that a further employment investigation is not required. Indeed, it is best to keep the prospect of disciplinary action out of the investigation in the early stages. Employees who consider that they may be facing disciplinary action will not be as open with the organisation and the key facts may not be identified as quickly as they otherwise would have been.

If the company does decide to take action against an individual, the usual HR process will need to be followed in order to reach a dismissal decision. The company may wish to consider litigation against the employee, but usually this will only be worthwhile if the employee has deep pockets.

REPORTING TO AND COOPERATION WITH LAW ENFORCEMENT AUTHORITIES

If the data breach has involved the unauthorised access or loss of personal data, the company will also need to consider its obligation to report to the relevant regulator. This should take place within the required 72 hour window, with as much detail as the company is able to provide. Other EU regulations, such as the Directive on Security of Network and Information Systems (NIS Directive), if applicable may provide even tighter reporting timeframes. The company will need to ensure that the regulator is updated as the investigation progresses and further detail is available. Should the breach present a high risk to the data subjects, the company will also need to notify the individuals of the incident and the possible risks to them, along with the suggested mitigation. The requirement to report externally highlights the need to both effectively investigate any breaches, but also to prevent them from happening in the first place.

Depending on the particular nature of the incident, it may also be worth considering involving law enforcement authorities. For example, the UK's National Crime Agency and Germany's PPO enjoy wide search and seizure powers. If a crime has been committed they may be better placed to act quickly to contain an incident and/or to secure evidence using these powers. The civil option may be more time consuming and would certainly be more expensive (for the employer who will bear the legal costs) than action taken by law enforcement. Involving law enforcement can also play well to the communications narrative for the employer, demonstrating that they are taking the incident extremely seriously. However, consideration also needs to be given to the fact that involving law enforcement necessarily leads to a loss of control over what may be a key part of the investigation. In Germany, where the PPO is involved it is a mandatory requirement to conduct any further investigation (especially interviews with suspects including employees) in close coordination with the PPO. Where a crime has been committed, the employer should also check whether there are any mandatory obligations to report the offence to local law enforcement which is required in some jurisdictions.

CONCLUSION

Insider threat is a critical issue for all organisations and one which poses significant risks – including loss of data, reputational damage, financial liability and potential regulatory fines. Insiders may act maliciously, but often can be acting by accident or otherwise innocently. As with all enterprise risk, preventing these risks is better than seeking to mend any damage already caused. In order to do this, rigorous and thorough data protection policies and controls are required together with regular table top exercises to "normalise" incident response and train up crisis response teams. If a breach does occur, it is important to ensure that the response is appropriate in the circumstances. However, given the need to carefully balance the rights of employees against these risks to the business, implementing an insider threat programme cannot be successful without careful consideration of the legal and regulatory implications.

8

FROM SECURITY AWARENESS TRAINING TO SECURE BEHAVIOUR CHANGE

TIM WARD AND MIKE BUTLER, THINK CYBER SECURITY LTD

Training, education and awareness are vital in any information security strategy since security is frequently weak at the end-user level, and personnel are often not aware of security policies and standards[1]. Furthermore, a security awareness program is a requirement in an increasing number of standards and regulations, including ISO27001, PCI DSS and COBIT[2]. To address this need, the market for Security Awareness products has existed in a recognisable form for more than ten years[3].

Until very recently, however, Security Awareness solutions have focussed almost exclusively on 'training' end-users rather than on what is arguably needed: changing end-user security behaviour (which we term Secure Behaviour Change). Perhaps it is because compliance with standards and regulations can foster a 'tick-box' approach to fulfilling requirements, but the success criteria for awareness initiatives commonly takes the form of "have I delivered training to end-users?" rather than "have I changed the security behaviour of end-users (and therefore reduced the risk to my organisation)?".

How, though, do we approach behaviour change in a security context? How do we understand the decisions end-users make; and how do we take steps to influence them? Behaviour change models that combine insights from the fields of psychology (the science of behaviour and mind) and behavioural economics (the study of economic decision making and choice) are a good place to start.

1. ISACA, CISM Review Manual, 14th Edition, pp.65.
2. Security Awareness Compliance Requirements, SANS Institute https://www.sans.org/sites/default/files/2017-12/sans-compliance-requirements.pdf
3. Gartner Security Awareness Magic Quadrant, 2018

1. BEHAVIOUR CHANGE MODELS

Standard economic theory used to hold sway in its suggestion that we make decisions in a purely rational, selfish, way. It is now well established that the reality is somewhat more complicated than that. Over the last two decades, psychology and, in particular, behavioural economics have been popularised by researchers such as Kahneman[4] and Thaler/Sunstein[5] – with Kahneman and Thaler both having received Nobel prizes for their contributions. More recently, the application of insights from these fields to the types of habit-forming technology that Silicon Valley produces has garnered attention[6].

Drawing on psychology and behavioural economics, behaviour change models attempt to explain how and why behaviours change. Noting that they are an intentional simplification, or abstraction, of the many complexities of human cognition, such models provide useful frameworks for both understanding behaviour and delivering behavioural interventions. In the context of Secure Behaviour Change, two such models are particularly thought provoking:

- *Protection Motivation Theory* – originated by R.W.Rogers[7] as a way of clarifying and understanding how people cope with "fear appeals" – that is, the way in which fear works to motivate behaviour (see Fig. 8.1.)
- *Fogg Behavior Model* – proposed by Stanford Professor BJ Fogg[8] as a model for understanding human behaviour in order to analyse and design persuasive technologies (see Fig. 8.2.)

Figure 8.1 – Protection Motivation Theory

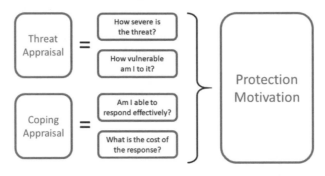

Protection Motivation Theory

4. Kahneman, D. (2011). Thinking, fast and slow. New York: Farrar, Straus and Giroux
5. Thaler, R. H., & Sunstein, C. R. (2009). Nudge: improving decisions about health, wealth, and happiness.
6. Eyal, N. (2014). Hooked: how to build habit-forming products.
7. Rogers R.W. (1975) A protection motivation theory of fear appeals and attitude change. Journal of Psychology, 91, 93-114
8. BJ Fogg. 2009. A behavior model for persuasive design. In Proceedings of the 4th International Conference on Persuasive Technology (Persuasive '09). ACM, New York, NY, USA, Article 40, 7 pages

Protection Motivation Theory suggests that an individual will make two assessments (or 'appraisals') when making a decision under threat. The first assesses the threat in terms of perceived severity and their perceived vulnerability to it. The second assesses capacity to cope with the threat in terms of their ability to respond effectively, and also the cost of making that response. Note that these appraisals should not be equated purely to deliberate thought processes that are invoked by a threat – but rather should be considered to encompass immediate, instinctive, reactions as well as more deliberate reasoning.

This model emphasises the need for behaviour change initiatives to encompass both elements, coping as well as threat, in order to persuade people to make effective decisions. It is not only necessary to convey the threats that exist, and how those threats can cause harm, but also to provide mechanisms for responding easily and effectively to those threats.

Figure 8.2 – Fogg Behavior Model

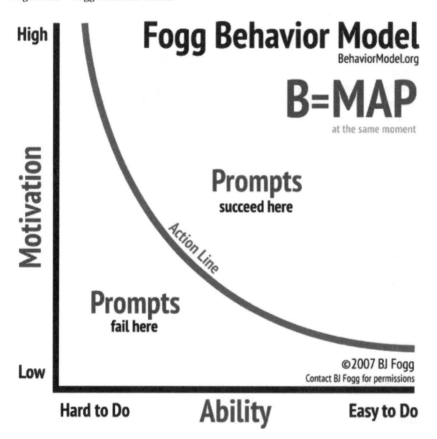

Fogg Behavior Model (behaviormodel.org) – reproduced with permission

Fogg's model describes three components:

- Motivation – is the target of my behaviour change initiative sufficiently motivated to change their behaviour?
- Ability – does my target have the capability to undertake the required behaviour modification?
- Prompt – is my target suitably prompted to effect the required behaviour change?

These three components are plotted on the above graph, with Ability and Motivation on the x- and y-axis respectively. The curved line represents the point at which the desired behaviour change action occurs, with Prompting activities failing when the Motivation versus Ability point is positioned below the line and succeeding when it falls above it.

The following points are particularly noteworthy:

- End-users need to be both Motivated and Able to perform our desired behaviour. The more motivated they are to undertake an activity, the harder they are prepared to work for it; and the easier an activity is to perform, the less motivation is required.
- It is necessary to Prompt users to make desired changes. Fogg argues that persuasion towards behaviour change will fail unless all three components are present. End-users must have just enough of both Motivation and Ability to push them across the line to where Prompts to change will be effective. Fogg highlights three different types of Prompt – a 'spark' (a trigger which motivates behaviour), a 'facilitator' (which makes the target behaviour easier) or a 'signal' (which indicates or reminds) – and notes that sparks and facilitators are the most effective.
- In order to prevent a behaviour from occurring, Fogg suggests taking away one of the three factors: reducing motivation, taking away ability, or removing triggers. However, he also notes that designing systems to prevent behaviours is generally more difficult than making behaviours happen.

2. APPLYING THE MODELS TO SECURITY

Before considering how these models may be applied to the security context, it is worth pausing to consider two key constraints:

1. Security is not necessarily something the individuals want to learn about.
2. Nor is acting securely their primary task on a day to day basis.

The challenge is therefore to impart awareness, education, knowledge and ideally change behaviours in a context where the user's attention needs to be grabbed and coerced into the required behaviour.

2.1 APPLYING PROTECTION MOTIVATION THEORY

Considering the theory against our experience of current approaches to security awareness, it is notable that:

- Current approaches often focus primarily on the threat and do too little to address effective and actionable coping mechanisms.
- Over-complex security instructions may even risk negatively impacting people's perception of their ability to make good decisions, whilst also increasing their perception of the cost (in other words 'effort') of doing the right thing.

In short, getting the approach and emphasis wrong risks removing people's motivation to do the right thing – increasing the likelihood that they just, for example, cross their fingers, click a link and plead ignorance after the fact!

So, what does this mean for practitioners developing security awareness training courses? The theory would suggest the following:

- *Just enough 'threat'*. It is important that people have enough of an appreciation of the threat for coping mechanisms to come into play. After all, if people do not recognise they are under threat, a coping mechanism is irrelevant. But not to overdo it, and to also make sure people understand how they personally are vulnerable.
- *Make it actionable*. Ensure that information about the threat is accompanied by practical 'coping' information about steps people can take to deal with it. As a basic example in the context of phishing, simply encourage people, if they're not sure about an email, to consult colleagues or those with expert knowledge (if present in the organisation). Alternatively, ask people to take simple steps to verify suspect emails – for example, by picking up the phone, or by logging into relevant accounts without acting on email links. A positive focus on coping, rather than trying to prevent a behaviour also aligns with Fogg's view that it is harder to prevent a behaviour than encourage a new one.
- *Keep it simple*. Ensure that security instructions are realistic and perceived as low cost, for the typical user. And make them memorable, aided by ongoing refreshers. Do not expect people to become security experts.

The focus should be on creating an enduring, but appropriate, level of security awareness. Practitioners should think hard about the degree of expertise they expect people to have and whether it is realistic; and then make sure it goes hand in hand with effective, simple and memorable coping mechanisms.

2.2 APPLYING THE FOGG BEHAVIOR MODEL

The challenging context for Security Awareness has already been noted: we are trying to educate users on a topic they may well not be interested in. Now when considering Fogg's model, we can see that we are likely starting at the bottom of the Motivation curve. A Prompt will always be required, but the action must also be easy to get the desired behaviour. This clearly aligns with Protection Motivation Theory highlighting that the focus should be on a simple, actionable coping behaviour rather than 'education' per se.

Looking at one aspect of Security Awareness, strong and separate passwords, through the lens of the Fogg Behavior Model is informative. It is a typical requirement of organisational security policy that users should adopt passwords that are both strong (i.e. hard to guess) and separate (i.e. not used elsewhere). What does Fogg's model tell us about how to persuade people to do so?

Considering Ability
There is a clear implication that the easier it can be made to perform the target behaviour, the better. Asking users to set and remember (potentially numerous) long strings of random characters which change every few months is not easy. That is why the NCSC now recommends not requiring frequent password changes, forming passwords from three random words, and say that password managers are a "good thing". All measures that push password policy compliance away from being "hard-to-do" and towards being "easy-to-do". This could be taken even further by providing tools for users, for example offering a widget that helps them see how to generate secure passwords[910].

Considering Motivation
The most important thing to recognise here is that Motivation is something that needs to be considered!

All-to-often in Security Awareness, Motivation is neglected, and users are expected to just "do their training". Fogg describes the core human motivators as being pleasure/pain, hope/fear and social acceptance/rejection. It appears that the default position with Security Awareness is to leverage fear ("if you do not do X, attackers will steal all your data") and pain ("if you do not do Y, access will be revoked") as core motivators. However, it is worth considering social acceptance ("others are doing this, join the party") as a more positive way of increasing Motivation.

Considering Prompts
Again, the primary thing to note is that appropriate Prompts need to be considered!

Behaviour change does not just happen by magic because the security team desire it. In fact, it is underpinned by providing the user with the right cue at the right time (the "opportune moment") to undertake the target behaviour. Whilst it is true that Prompts do not work if Motivation and Ability are not squared away, it is notable that Prompts are almost entirely absent from Security Awareness.

When it comes to passwords, behaviour change will not simply happen by making people aware of password policy on an annual basis via mandatory training: annual training is just about the worst Prompt for action one can imagine. So, when is the opportune moment to trigger behaviour change around password policy? What about when people are changing their password?

9. https://www.ncsc.gov.uk/blog-post/three-random-words-or-thinkrandom-0
10. https://www.ncsc.gov.uk/blog-post/what-does-ncsc-think-password-managers

Prompts can be tuned through understanding interactions between aspects of Fogg's model. For example, Fogg notes that "easy-to-do" or simplicity is a function of a person's scarcest resource *at the moment a behaviour is triggered*. If users are left to set passwords at the last minute, then time is likely to be scarce. Rushing may result in a simple incremental change to their last password. If a timely Prompt for action is delivered when the user's password is nearly due for renewal, then their memory for the password might become the scarcest resource, but one that can be alleviated by the three random words technique or a password manager.

BUILDING HABITS

BJ Fogg has built his theory into a 'Tiny Habits' program[11] and highlights how successful organisations such as Facebook, Google, Instagram, Twitter have made fortunes with techniques that turn the use of their products into automatic habits[12]. Applying this to security awareness suggests that once we have driven a simple behaviour, we can start to move up the curve, to do something a bit harder. In the context of phishing, rather than starting by trying to train our staff on how to spot phishing, we could follow the steps below:

- Start by encouraging staff to be vigilant, cautious and suspicious and report anything they aren't sure of – a simple, easy and low-cost coping behaviour, and a measurable one.
- Play back these reported emails as a 'reward' and to highlight reporting as a 'social norm' to increase motivation.
- As reporting levels increase, start to build up skills in spotting key features of phishing, by showing examples of attacks ranging from basic through to sophisticated.

SUMMARY

In this short chapter we have explored the potential to transition from security *awareness* to *secure behaviour change*. The initial driver for Security Awareness was as a means to an end, to reduce risk and prevent security incidents. Over time it has become the end in its own right, to meet compliance requirements; with the secure behaviour change that it was really there to deliver perceived as too hard.

We have highlighted two, among many, theories of behaviour change: BJ Fogg's Behavior Change Model and Protection Motivation Theory. Fogg's model suggesting the need to consider Motivation, Ability and a Prompt to act; and Protection Motivation Theory suggesting the need to think about coping mechanism as well as threat. We have then demonstrated how these two models can be applied to the delivery of security awareness, both focusing the content to make it simple, actionable and with

11. https://www.tinyhabits.com
12. https://www.forbes.com/sites/anthonykosner/2012/12/04/stanfords-school-of-persuasion-bj-fogg-on-how-to-win-users-and-influence-behavior/#45551931390d

just enough threat; as well as making the behaviour easy, motivating the targets using cognitive biases such as social acceptance, and most importantly delivering a timely prompt to act.

ThinkCyber are a Cyber Security start-up focusing on delivering pragmatic, user centric solutions to cyber security challenges. Working alongside academics from UCL and Northumbria University and with InnovateUK support, they have created their RedFlags™ product. A software toolkit designed to drive secure behaviour change by delivering ongoing and timely security awareness interventions across a range of threats from phishing to data handling, as well as providing security teams with full visibility of user engagement, completion rates, content dwell times and risky behaviours.

*ThinkCyber partner with AXELOS RESILIA, together empowering your users to protect themselves against cyber threats. Find out more at **thinkcyber**.co.uk.*

9

FIXING YOUR CYBERSECURITY STAFF RETENTION PROBLEM

KARLA REFFOLD, BEECHERMADDEN

THE WAR FOR COMPETITION IS HEATING UP

The prediction is now that there will be 3 million unfilled cybersecurity vacancies by 2022. It is well known that there is a shortage of cybersecurity staff globally and all organisations are feeling the effect of this. Companies are being forced to pay larger basic salaries for people, in order to attract them from competitors. Where possible, companies are relocating people, either within the same country or from overseas. There is a limit to this however. Companies can not be expected to continue to increase salaries and spend just to attract people to work for them. Companies have to work incredibly hard to retain the people they have, while attracting the new people they need. The only way to do this, is to understand what is important to your team, and what attracts them to your competition.

Retaining cybersecurity staff is an issue facing all companies with cybersecurity teams.
- In the UK, the average turnover rate for staff is 15%[1]
- In the cybersecurity industry, 40% moved jobs in the past 12 months
- 79% say they would consider moving jobs in the next 12 months
- Of those that moved jobs, 37% found a new role in less than 2 weeks

---

1. Source monster.co.uk

CAREER PROGRESSION IS THE NUMBER ONE REASON FOR MOVING JOBS

THE DEFINITION OF CAREER PROGRESSION IN CYBERSECURITY

In the 6 years I have been surveying candidates, the number one reason they give for wanting a new role is career progression. This features higher than the desire for a pay increase. Career progression is a broad phrase that can mean different things for different people and companies.

- There is no opportunity for promotion due to company structure
- A promotion opportunity exists but not for this candidate
- There is no perceived opportunity to be challenged further in the existing role
- The opportunity to develop further skills is not perceived to exist
- Progression does not always mean promotion

For smaller teams or organisations, it is unrealistic to expect significant opportunities for promotion or growth within the role. Many cyber teams are now large, and are often part of large global organisations. The opportunity for development and advancement exists within these organisations but the perception of this, is not always there. Cybersecurity is relatively new for many companies and there is not an industry defined route for career advancement.

HOW TO OFFER CAREER PROGRESSION

Offer training budgets

Companies that are doing well on retention and attraction, offer their staff training budgets. They can use this to further develop their skills or gain qualifications. This training can help make them more valuable to their organisation, either because they can be billed at a higher rate or can achieve better results in their role. Staff feel valued and developed, especially when they have control over how this money is spent. They are less likely to leave, not just because they feel that they are progressing, but because they are concerned about losing this benefit in going to another organisation.

If a training budget is not possible, then consider allowing employees paid time off to undertake further study or development at their own cost. This may involve going to conferences or doing further qualifications that they have paid for. If there is no financial support for this training, employees at least do not have to sacrifice annual leave or pay, to undertake further development.

Allow the opportunity to diversify their role

Where possible, allowing staff to increase their responsibility in their current role can help retain them. This may benefit the business by opening up security to different areas of the business. Perhaps a security risk manager can become more involved with the development process? This helps fill a DevSecOps gap and allows that employee to develop new skills. Can your security engineers take on more responsibility that delivers increased security to the company?

If promotion opportunities exist, highlight this
Candidates who understand what they need to do to advance, are more satisfied than those who do not have clear targets. This may involve staying in a similar role but being promoted to a higher grade, with more oversight. Or this may involve being promoted to a different role. As an industry, we can do more to show obvious career paths to the top but some of this will start with organisations developing their own plans. Make sure any roles are advertised internally so that employees feel they have a fair opportunity to apply and achieve promotions.

Have regular one to ones
Communication plays a large role in retention and development. While most large organisations have a mandated appraisal process to be followed, managers do not always take this seriously. 121's or appraisals are often seen as a box to be ticked, rather than a valuable retention tool. Making sure these form a regular part of your people management, can help with career progression. This gives you an opportunity to explain to your staff what skills they are lacking, that is preventing them from progressing. You can also help them with a plan on how to develop these skills. It is an opportunity for them to raise their concerns with you, and an opportunity for you to fix it before they decide to look at external opportunities.

PASSIONS PROJECTS ARE A KEY RETENTION TOOL

PROJECT WORK HELPS WITH PROGRESSION AND JOB SATISFACTION

Employees who have a real passion for the job and work on projects in their spare time are the most sought-after. They can demonstrate commitment to their work, and that shows through in an interview. These are the employees who are going to find a way to fix the problem because that's what they love. They are going to innovate and find better solutions.

Helping them feed that passion benefits everyone. The business gets employees with constantly developing skills who may even find a solution with a business benefit. What we hear from these select few, time and time again, is that they don't want to move jobs because they don't think another employer will give them time for these projects. They are happy and motivated.

This retention tactic is also an attraction tactic. Giving employees this time can be added to a job advert or job description. It can also be made conditional on having achieved certain metrics, if there is a concern that core activities will suffer as a result. These passion projects also help with the career development problem. Employees can feel that they are developing and progressing in the career without moving jobs.

HOW TO OFFER PASSION PROJECTS

Passion projects will differ from role. That they are "passion" projects means they will differ between individuals. There are some ideas that you could consider, per job role.

- Penetration testers may be excited by the idea of testing the security of different products. Rather than trying to break into a company, if they can have time to try and break into IoT products, they may be more satisfied in their job.
- Information risk managers may like the idea of working on solutions for new risks or working in newer areas of the business. Putting them into a DevSecOps role would allow them to work in a new area and help with the considerable skills gap in development teams.
- Consultants may want to look at a project with a client in an industry which the business hasn't worked in before. This may start with researching the industry or attending events, and develop into a new revenue stream for the business.

MAKE SURE CYBERSECURITY IS TAKEN SERIOUSLY BY THE BUSINESS

STAFF FEEL FRUSTRATED WHEN THEY CAN'T MAKE A DIFFERENCE

The best cybersecurity employees are really engaged with the industry and they look externally to find better solutions or to spot trends. If the trend they spot is that their organization is behind or not taking cybersecurity seriously, they will be tempted to move on. These candidates want to effect real change and do a good job. When they are prevented from doing that, they will become frustrated. This doesn't mean having the newest tools, or the biggest budgets, but it does mean fixing known vulnerabilities and having a leadership team that is committed to embedding security.

At the current time, people are the key focus for cybersecurity, in the triumvirate of people, process and technology. Effecting cultural change amongst the people in the wider business, is driven by senior leadership taking security seriously. Your staff won't stop leaving their passwords under their keyboard, if their director does the same (although GDPR has massively helped with this). Cybersecurity needs to be driven by the leadership exhibiting the right behaviours, so that everyone else follows. If your cybersecurity staff do not see this from their leadership, their efforts are being frustrated and they will look to move on to a company where they can make a difference.

NO ONE EXPECTS AN UNLIMITED BUDGET

Much in cybersecurity comes back to budgets. For good, or even adequate cybersecurity, there needs to be an appropriate spend. But ensuring the organisation is taking security seriously does not mean that employees expect an unlimited amount of spend. Those working in the NHS for example, are aware that money spent on technology takes money away from patients. What is important, is that budget is given for key, basic measures so that there is core level of security. For staff to feel that security is being taken seriously, they need to feel that budget is granted for recommendations they make and that the response is appropriate. If budget is continually denied for key security measures, employees will go elsewhere. If budget is denied for measures that provide advanced security, or for new innovations, employees will be understanding as long as the explanation is made clear by their leadership.

STRONG LEADERSHIP IS IMPORTANT FOR RETENTION

Ensuring the business takes cybersecurity seriously is often the responsibility of the CISO. Having a strong, well-respected CISO makes a large difference for staff retention. A CISO who understands the business and can present well to the board, will gain the right budget and buy-in, to make sure the whole business is taking cybersecurity seriously. Not only would the CISO be able to effect the team receiving adequate budget, but they will be able to explain to the team why some suggestions have not been taken on board. Helping the team understand how budget is being spent and when they can expect to embed newer processes, will mean the team can still feel as though the business is taking security seriously.

A well-respected CISO has an effect that is bigger than gaining budget and communicating security, both up and down. Having a boss you enjoy working for resonates with everyone, not just those in cybersecurity. One of the nuances of cybersecurity is that some have risen to management very quickly, often as a result of being the only person available to promote. Providing strong leadership to your team really helps employees feel connected to the vision of the business and builds a connection for them in their role. A cybersecurity leader who is active on the speaking circuit or is seen in the industry as a thought leader will make your employees proud to be a part of your team.

SALARY MATTERS, BUT IT'S NOT THE ONLY ANSWER

IT PAYS TO MOVE ON

In our 2019 salary survey (see Fig. 9.1 and 9.2 below), BeecherMadden asked what pay rise cybersecurity professionals achieved if they stayed with their organisation and what they achieved if they left. 39% of those who moved externally achieved a pay rise of 26% or higher. 36% of those who stayed with their organisation, received no pay rise. When changing that percentage increase to just 10%, the numbers are even more stark. Only 28% of those who stayed with their organisation received a pay rise of over 10%. 71% of those who moved, received an increase over 10%.

Figure 9.1 – Pay increase achieved on moving externally

Figure 9.2 – Pay increase achieved last year in staying

REVIEW SALARIES REGULARLY

Paying candidates more money is not a quick fix to the retention problem. Companies are often restrained by pay grades internally. Continually increasing salaries to keep up with competitors is not necessarily the right commercial decision. However, monitoring the market and ensuring you are not falling too far behind may stop this before it becomes a problem. Waiting until someone leaves to pay them more is often fraught with problems.

Employees do question why they had to look elsewhere before you decided to pay them more money. Candidates are wary of counter-offers and it is far more successful to ensure appropriate remuneration before you are forced to.

YOU DON'T NEED TO PAY THE MOST

Your employees are almost certainly being approached about other opportunities every day. For those with in-demand technical skills, this may be multiple times in a day. Most of these approaches will be offering them a higher salary. Candidates are bored of these approaches. They will become fatigued with considering other opportunities. While longevity in a role is not valued that highly in the current market, it is a consideration. What we see, is that it is rarely just money that inspires candidates to consider another opportunity. As long as you are close to market rate, you do not have to be the highest payer to retain your staff. You need the right environment for your team, more than you need to continually increase pay.

CONCLUSION

Employee retention is a complex issue and the solution for each person will be slightly different. Cybersecurity has some unique challenges for organisations at present. Cybersecurity departments are relatively new to the business landscape and as such, they are not well understood by HR or the wider organisation. The huge demand for these skills provides a different challenge that is not seen in more traditional departments. Some of the retention solutions can be applied to all areas of the business and some will need to be tailored to this industry differently. Considering the key points of career progression, passion projects, strong leadership and salary will help you retain your team. What is key, is communicating with your team, making them feel valued and implementing a retention strategy before you have a retention problem.

10

HOW TO SECURE, PROTECT AND BUILD RESILIENCE

MAUREEN KENDAL, CYBERCARE LTD

Resilience is the capacity to recover quickly from difficult challenges. The National Crime Agency places building resilience in the community as their Key Performance Question 6[1]. Resilience in the community relies on the interrelationship between government and individuals, families and groups. Individuals need to respect and take responsibility for the protection of lives and ownership of property and information. Often systems go wrong, people make mistakes. People and information become vulnerable to abuse.

In order to build resilience and combat Cyber Risk in our IT lifestyle, we need to understand how our IT systems can be vulnerable and open to risk. If we are not aware of our potential vulnerabilities we cannot protect ourselves or bounce back after attack. To keep our IT systems as safe as possible, we need to assess what, who and where to trust.

Imagine our non-digital world; what does Trust feel like in this non-digital world? We are at home. It's a Sunday, we are relaxed in weekend loafing clothes, we place our secret diary, our personal photos, our intimate symbolic objects in our top drawer. We put our valuables somewhere safe, accessible and near us. We hide our most valuable items in a security box, under the floorboards, in a bank vault, or maybe in a not-to-be-used special sock in our sock drawer. Later in the evening, we get dressed in our smart casuals and we invite trusted friends over and share a meal or go out for some drinks and tell them a joke or about a funny, slightly embarrassing incident. On Monday, we go out in our work clothes, we put on our coats, umbrellas, hooded jackets or

---

1. The National Crime Agency – Annual Plan 2018-2019. KPQ6. p18.

sunglasses. These clothes and accessories signal our status, our social or religious tribe, the type of work, and they might shield us against the weather. We lock our home, its windows and doors, maybe put on our alarm system. At work or with people we meet in the street or at public events, we may not share our intimate, sensitive or embarrassing images or stories. We make judgements, when and with whom, we share different types of information.

We make decisions on how open or restricted we create our communication boundaries. Our non-digital physical world offers us choices. We base these choices on our perception of trust and identities. We use keys, locations and decoys to hide, obscure or to securely mark and identify valuables. We judge whom we might trust, then decide on what to tell and what not to say. We might reveal unique or sensitive information whilst seeking to belong to a specific group, as part of socialising empathising behaviour – 'I too am like you or I am not like you.' Why do we share sensitive communication? Why do we trust or mis-trust? We trust, love, cherish and empathise with others because, as babies and children, we were able to bond with our care-givers and trust them to love us, feed us and protect us. We trust because we are human. Trust enables us to survive, create and procreate in the physical world. Validating trust and trusted communication channels is essential to being safe online.

OUR RIGHT TO USE THE INTERNET SAFELY?

Being secure online and mindful of cybersecurity is now part of human rights and responsibilities[2]. We navigate our way through our lives, balancing our ability to empathise and our ability to make sound judgements. We seek to communicate: to belong to our social or interest group, tribe, geographical region, to understand our narratives. Who are we? What are our values? What are our expectations? What can we contribute to our communities? How can we put bread on the table and shelter over our heads? How can we make relationships and build family structures? However we navigate our worlds, we need to be connected online, locally and globally. Today we cannot be active and contributing citizens without being online. This is a human right. Legally, we are entitled to expect access to the internet and have global reach into an extensive knowledge base. Amber Rudd's announcement in April 2018 indicates that the government is providing a £9 million fund available to law enforcement to tackle those who use the anonymity of online space for illegal activities such as the selling of firearms, drugs, malware and people. £5 million will be used to support the police to establish dedicated cyber crime units. This is a step towards cyber safety. CyberCare's cost assessment of a necessary and significant shift indicates that this is insufficient. A comprehensive approach needs to encompass cyber education, culture and technology. Requirements are cyber awareness training, early intervention flagging up potential incidents, crisis intervention and sustainable structures within

---

2. Declaration of Human Rights Article 27. http://www.unesco.org/culture/culture-sector-knowl-edge-management-tools/11_InfoSheet_CulturalRights.pdf

our communities. This comprehensive approach is needed to keep on top of the cyber challenges that are evolving and emerging.[3]

BEING ONLINE – EDUCATION, CULTURE, TECHNOLOGY

We need to be educated to make judgements on how to be safe. Culturally, we have social identities, we present social and business selves in specific ways, we need to consider what may be sensitive information. Technically, to protect ourselves, we may use decoys or safety locks, trusted certificates and personal identities.

We can use education, culture and technology to build an online world which offers ways to trust and empower us. We need to know who to trust and how this can be validated across different scenarios.

IT systems are enabled by many layers within the communication network. As we use the IT system, trusted pathways within each layer need to be validated. Cyber-Education needs to build IT knowledge and skills integrated with roles, responsibilities and citizenship. Cyber-Culture needs to enable dialogue between generations, cultures and other digital divides. Dialogue that promotes caring, sharing, creativity and business exchange yet is protected by legal boundaries. Cyber-Technology can be understood as a systematic, comprehensive framework. IT is not simply a product e.g. iPhone or a community such as Facebook, but is a complex system with access points, layers, components, connectivity and code. This three-pronged approach of education, culture and technology, underpins specialist advice and government intervention. The approach is not new; ten years ago, the Byron Review sought to safeguard children in the online environment[4], through improved legal regulation, education, classification reform and technical safety settings.

IF WE USE ESSENTIAL SAFETY GUIDELINES, HOW SAFE ARE WE?

Fear of using the internet stems from a basic lack of knowledge, from being a target of a common scam or from unusual or abusive targeted malicious personalised attacks.

There are common safeguards which the public are advised to take on board. The National Centre for Cybersecurity offers online resources aimed at business users – Cyber Essentials.[5]

These are:
1. Firewalls
2. Security settings

---

3. cybercare.org.uk, April 2018;
https://www.enterprisetimes.co.uk/2018/04/12/amber-rudd-announces-crackdown-on-dark-web
4. The Byron Review, June 2008.
Safer Children in a Digital World: The Report of the Byron Review
https://webarchive.nationalarchives.gov.uk/20100202110916/http://www.dcsf.gov.uk/byronreview
NSPCC (2017) Ten years since the Byron Review: are children safer in the digital world? London: NSPCC.
https://learning.nspcc.org.uk/research-resources/2018/10-years-since-the-byron-review/
5. https://www.cyberessentials.ncsc.gov.uk.

3. Controlled access
4. Protection against malware
5. Updating your devices

Their guides for small business users advocate these five steps. [6] The hope is that this awareness will filter down from small business users to the individual, families and the communities. In many cases this may occur, but the majority of individuals at home and out and about are still at risk. For households, families and individual users, we advocate these Cyber Essentials.

CYBER ESSENTIALS

1. Back up
2. Update all devices and software and protect against malware using anti-virus software
3. Control access by using passwords and authentication and where possible firewalls
4. Use closed and secured networks
5. Beware of scams, spoofing, spam and phishing.

Anti-virus software protects about 30-40% of known hacks. 60-70% of reported cybercrime can be minimised by using these Cyber Security Essentials. However, 20% of hacks are more complex to defend and protect. Abusive targeted malicious personalised attacks are difficult complex challenges and account for only 0.5-2.5% of all reported hacks.

Most individuals, most of the time, if they use these common Cyber Security Essentials, can use the internet safely without fear.

6. Cyber Security Small Business Guide and Infographic, www.ncsc.gov.uk/small business. 2017

PART THREE

CULTURAL ISSUES AND BOTTOM LINE IMPACT

11

TRUST ISSUES CAN BE GOOD

HOW ADOPTING A ZERO-TRUST POSTURE CAN IMPROVE YOUR SECURITY

NICK IOANNOU, BOOLEAN LOGICAL

In today's online world, trust takes on a whole new dimension that we have not been psychologically prepared for as a society, and the cyber criminals exploit this to their advantage.

Trust is something we are born with; we trust our parents, our extended family, our teachers and friends, unless we experience anything contrary to this. As we grow older, we learn to trust the government, banks, our employers, as well as major utility suppliers and large companies. We expect them to operate within the law and apply the safeguards of regulations. Yet this trust is what is being used to bypass much of our cyber security systems.

Society is based on trust, otherwise everything rapidly descends to anarchy. We quickly develop trust relationships with people, organisations and even brands, based on our positive experiences normally with some form of visual or physical confirmation. The trust the bank teller because we have walked into a building with the right logos and branding for our particular bank. The bank teller will be wearing a uniform or badge and will typically be on the other side of the counter that we are not allowed into. Now that many of us do our banking online, we don't walk into a building and we don't see anyone who works for the bank. Instead we visit a website or launch a mobile app and trust what we see.

We recognise people, logos and brands, yet online this recognition can be easily tricked. We assume high levels of security when in fact the walls are paper thin. Or more importantly, we could think we were somewhere legitimate online, but actually tricked into being somewhere fake. Now in the physical world you would need to go to the lengths taken in the TV series *Mission Impossible* from the 1960s to trick someone into thinking they had walked into a bank, when in fact it is completely fake. Online though it is a different matter as it takes little effort in comparison to create a convincing clone of any website. The problem isn't just online though, many scams are also perpetrated via phone calls, text messages, and social media, as well as online.

The phone scams have been running for the best part of two decades, with slight modifications to the script to keep the scam plausible as technology moves on. The initial premise is often the same, that your internet service provider or Microsoft has detected something malicious on your computer. Next follows a guided walkthrough to convince you that their claim is genuine. It's all smoke and mirrors though, relying on the limited computer knowledge of the average user to trick them. The next step is normally to establish a remote access connection via legitimate systems such as LogMeIn Rescue, by asking you to visit http://www.logmein123.com and enter a six-digit code. This is the same system that is actually used by Microsoft at https://support.microsoft.com/help to resolve technical issues for paid support and services. Once you have given the scammer remote access, they then proceed to transfer and run malicious files onto your machine or pretend to fix the issue. During the remote access session, the question of the cost crops up where they ask you for a serious amount of money to fix the issue or offer you an annual support subscription normally to the tune of £195 or more. Either way, your computer will probably be compromised when it never originally was, and the criminals now have your payment card information and more.

Text message scammers can cause even more havoc, because through flaws in the technology, messages appear to be from institutions and organisations we trust. These fake messages appear in the same grouping as the legitimate ones still stored on our phones. We automatically assume the message to be genuine because it has come from the correct number, and we know the number is correct from all the previous messages. So, the alert to say "call this number as we have discovered a discrepancy in your last tax return" is not questioned. You ring the number and answer the security questions as expected. Unfortunately, when asked to confirm a bank account or debit card to get the supposed refund, the joy and expectation of this unexpected windfall outweighs the normal reservations people would have.

Text message scams may not be trying to get you to ring a telephone number though, often they just contain a website link, for which the scammers know that there is a high probability that you will view them on a mobile. If you are ever taken to website via a text message that then asks you for login credentials, assume the link is fake and ideally using a different computer to visit the organisation concerned by either manually typing in the address or using an existing bookmark. Don't let time pressure get the better of you; if you can, wait until you can manually type the correct address of the website concerned on a computer or laptop.

It doesn't help that we have no easy and quick way of verifying who someone is in a phone call, or a text message. If the criminals manage to spoof the genuine numbers, then we assume it is real and answer the security questions as expected. But we are allowed to challenge the caller; in fact the caller really needs to verify themselves to you first, before you give any personal or financial information away. They contacted you after all, yet they treat it like you called them. While they cannot give away personal information, they can validate themselves through information only the valid organisation would know about you or your account. They can also give you tiny snippets of things like the third and eighth letter of your password. Occasionally the person you are speaking to refuses to validate themselves; so instead the best course of action is to ask for their name and department so you can call them back. It is then a case of searching for their number online so you can call them back. The is no point asking for their number or calling them on the number they called you on, in case they turn out not to be who they say they are.

Verifying emails takes things to a whole new level as the criminals have a wide array of techniques to try and fool us (illustrated in Figure. 11.1.) This can be as simple as the use of display name deception, as many smartphones hide the full email address, the use of a lookalike web domain to spoof the domain and change the 'from' entry in the email (because it turns out that email isn't actually secure), or just compromise the credentials of legitimate email accounts. Typically, this is achieved by phishing the email user, via data breaches or credential stuffing and is effectively the right car, but the wrong (fake) driver.

Figure 11.1 – E mail techniques that fool

	Display Name	From Email Address	Senders Actual Email
Display Name Deception	nick ioannou	nick123456_789@gmail.com	nick123456_789@gmail.com
Lookalike Domain	nick ioannou	info@boolean1ogical.com	info@boolean1ogical.com
Spoofed	nick ioannou	info@booleanlogical.com	nick123456_789@gmail.com
Compromised Credentials	nick ioannou	info@booleanlogical.com	info@booleanlogical.com

Spotting a compromised email can be incredibly challenging- the signature is more often than not, genuine. Technological solutions seldom help; so instead focus on the context. Is the way the email starts typical to how that person would write, is there a 'Dear…' when there never has been in the past? Is the file sharing link using a system they have used in the past? Is the attachment named how you would expect it to be or is it too vague? Is the attachment file type what you normally receive from them? Is the grammar and tone how you expect it to be? It is important to be slightly suspicious of every email that contains document links or attachments, because the sender may not be who you think it is. If anything looks slightly out of the ordinary, pause for thought and look for more clues. Telephone or text the person if you can from a number you already have for them and ask them if they have just sent you the email concerned. This is preferable to emailing them, because if their email account has been compromised, then the criminal could easily be the one replying.

Lookalike domains can contain numbers instead of letters like www.dropb0x.com but they can also contain international characters that for all intents and purposes, look exactly the same as the genuine domain. For example, the Latin small letter i with a grave looks like this: ì, or how about this Greek small letter NU: ν which looks just like a standard letter v. But many criminals don't go to the bother of registering new web domains though; instead they create subdomains that will appear in front of their domains containing trademarked and familiar companies and organisations. Web addresses can get ridiculously long with all sorts of gobbledygook meant for a computer, after the official web domain. We are so used to seeing the familiar bit near the front and often unintelligible characters afterwards, so it is quite easy to fool people so long as a recognisable web name is in a fake address. This also allows the criminals to target hundreds of different organisations using just one web domain, which often they don't even own themselves, but instead have obtained compromised admin credentials, through trickery or other means.

To protect yourself from falling for these fake subdomains, a good habit is to look for the two words either side of the last full stop in the first part of a web address, as this is the real web domain you are visiting. For example: https://www.britishairways.com/travel/managebooking/public/en_gb – in this legitimate British Airways website link, the two words either side of the last full stop are britishairways and com. While the last full stop in this similar looking fake https://www.britishairways.travllr.com/travel/managebooking/public/en_gb is actually between travllr and com. The second word after the last full stop is called a top-level domain (TLD) extension and the list of possibilities is currently at 1,578 words and growing, so it is not just .com, it could be .io, .xyz, .zone, as well as country codes like .uk or .eu.

Unfortunately, the criminals have a simple solution to stop you from seeing the real address in a web link by using a link shortener, this is basically a web link that automatically redirects to another web link. Link shorteners have lots of legitimate uses, I even use them myself via the bit.ly service to make it easier to share complex or overly long web pages, for example: http://bit.ly/HMRC-phishing-examples points to https://www.gov.uk/government/publications/phishing-and-bogus-emails-hm-revenue-and-customs-examples/phishing-emails-and-bogus-contact-hm-revenue-and-customs-examples which is a real mouthfull. Common link shorteners are: t.co, goo.gl, bit.ly, amzn.to, tinyurl.com, ow.ly, youtu.be, though there are many more. If you encounter a shortened link, the first question to ask yourself is why is this link shortened? Shortened links are meant for easy sharing, so anything personal doesn't need to be shortened. Luckily, there are free websites that can reveal where a shortened link goes, like http://checkshorturl.com/, https://unshorten.it/ and https://linkexpander.com/ though bear in mind the criminals can make a shortened link go to another shortened link and so on, which is an immediate red flag.

Another trick the criminals use is to embed the phishing or malicious link inside an Adobe PDF file or HTML file and then upload and share these via a legitimate file transfer or file sharing service such as Box, WeTransfer or Google Drive, to name a few. This means the email appears totally benign to most security solutions, so gets delivered as normal, unless it is blocked as spam. If you receive anything unexpected with a link to a file sharing service, assume it is fake or contact the sender if you know them. File transfer services are designed to handle extremely large files that email cannot, so if the file is tiny and easily sent as a normal email attachment, it is more than likely to be fake. If you need to check the file transfer service link, test it out on a mobile device, if it contains another link to go somewhere instead of an actual document, it's fake.

The best way to be safe is to never follow links and manually type in any web addresses as you expect them to be or use existing bookmarked addresses. Unfortunately, while this is good advice, it is no longer any guarantee when it comes to online shopping, as the criminals have a new opportunity to break our trust, one that has led to huge data breaches recently via a technique known as formjacking. By hacking particular elements of legitimate websites via their e-commerce plugins, the criminals can directly lift off all the information from the input fields where we enter our payment and address details. Formjacking takes theft to a new level as both the website owner and customer is completely oblivious that anything untoward has taken place, it is the online equivalent of a compromised payment card reader in a busy restaurant. To give you an idea of the scale of the problem, the antivirus company Symantec blocked over 3.7 million formjacking attempts in 2018, with over 50,000 online retailers affected. Your only defence is to limit the impact by only using credit cards or prepaid cards online, rather than debit cards and if you can, stick to a limited number of major online retailers as much as possible.

Lastly there's public wifi, whether in a train station, shopping centre or cafe, ask yourself if you actually need to use it, especially if you have a good mobile signal. It is very easy for criminals to set up a fake wifi hotspot, which allows to route all your online traffic through them, possibly capturing usernames, passwords and other information. Regardless of whether the wifi is real or fake, using public wifi means using someone else's internet connection; so it's best to avoid any online banking or shopping, as well as anything that you have to enter login credentials to access. Depending on how much monthly data you have included in your mobile contract, you could instead create a mobile hotspot from a smartphone if you need to connect a tablet device or laptop.

Ultimately, in all your communications and online dealings, a healthy habit of initial mistrust until you are satisfied someone or something can be trusted will greatly improve your overall security. If you are not sure about something, assume it is fake, especially for anything you received unexpectedly like a voucher, credit or prize, or anything claiming you need to confirm credentials to resolve a problem. The criminals will keep inventing new ways to attempt to trick us, but we can see through them, as trust needs to be earned.

12

CULTURE AND THE HUMAN FACTOR

CLOSING THE SECURITY SKILLS GAP BUILDS A BRIDGE TO THE FUTURE

STEVE DURBIN, INFORMATION SECURITY FORUM

In the normal day-to-day, it's easy to overlook our fragile dependence on the seamless digital infrastructure that supports our daily lives. Yet each time a major event occurs — natural disaster, widespread cyber-attack, government disruption, or massive breach of sensitive information — the visible and immediate impact on critical commercial, transportation, and public services is an eye-opening and timely reminder of our interconnectedness. In these moments of stark realization, the danger of understaffing critical cyber security programmes is impossible to dismiss. The more we transform our businesses, governments, and public and personal lives through digital technology and connectivity, the more we share the accompanying risks. The ancient adage seems timely once again: we're only as strong as the weakest link in the chain. And the security skills gap represents an alarmingly weak link.

In short, as the cyber threat landscape continues to grow more varied and intense in sophistication and strategic intent, the pressure on information security teams continues to mount. When a company doesn't have enough personnel to contain and understand the growing risks it faces, the struggle to hire and retain skill security professionals becomes a risk not only for that company, but also for any other entity connected to it.

THE EVOLUTION OF THE SECURITY WORKFORCE

The security workforce, typically defined as the personnel responsible for an organization's security activities, has evolved rapidly since its inception. The information security function, for example, often exists only as part of another associated business function, such as: risk, technical IT operations, legal and/or audit. Across various types of businesses and organizations, it carries many labels and falls under the purview of different units.

Over the course of its evolution, the lack of a consensus definition of the function has allowed numerous, disparate components to form an organization's security workforce. For example, employees working within threat intelligence, business continuity, and security operations are all essential information security contributors, yet they rarely convene in one distinct function under a designated leader.

SHORTFALLS IN SKILLS AND CAPABILITIES

Shortfalls in skills and capabilities have surely contributed to many of the major security incidents, data breaches, and ransomware attacks that have filled the headlines and resulted in widespread exposure of sensitive information, damage to brands and reputations, erosion of public trust, increased regulation, fraud and financial loss. Building tomorrow's security workforce is critical if we ever hope to see the day robust, efficient, and long-term enterprise security is normal and expected.

We've been talking about this skills shortage for many years now, at many levels of government, industry, and higher education. And yet, the gap persists. Organizations must commit to changing their attitude and approach to hiring and training, and step up their participation in joint pipeline development efforts. The traditional approach to identifying candidates is overly rigid. When combined with over-stressed and under-staffed work environments — not exactly appealing to the best candidates — this approach creates a funnel that is too narrow at the top. It's time to apply the creativity and passion for innovation that drove the meteoric rise of the digital economy to meeting this crucial challenge.

Filling the pipeline will require finding a way to channel the vast untapped pools of talent we know are out there. If only 20% of the global cybersecurity workforce is comprised of women, there are obviously lessons to be learned about how to attract bright prospects from a wider spectrum of education, experience, and expertise. It goes way beyond gender diversity; organizations must commit to developing initiatives aimed at fostering talent from younger and older age groups, underprivileged school districts, liberal arts colleges, and other "outside the box" options.

Organizations that fail to adopt a more creative approach will find themselves dangerously shorthanded in the next few years, as both attacks and defensive measures (e.g. security software platforms, patching and configuration practices, analytics, and machine learning initiatives) become more complex.

PAST: SECURITY IN SILOS

The security workforce, typically defined as the personnel responsible for an organization's information security activities, has evolved rapidly since its inception. The information security function often exists only as part of another associated business function, such as risk, technical IT operations, legal, or audit, and it might be called information, cyber, assurance, or operational security. It can also report into various business units, including finance, risk, governance, or IT.

Over time, the lack of a consensus definition or integrated structure has allowed numerous, disparate components to form the typical enterprise security workforce. It's shocking how rarely essential infosec contributors —employees working within threat intelligence, business continuity, and security operations — convene in one distinct function under a designated leader.

PRESENT: SUPPLY AND DEMAND ARE IMBALANCED

To have any hope of maintaining an effective security posture, enterprise executives must close the gap between supply and demand within their organization through a dynamic combination of workplace culture and appeal, strong processes and policies, and integrated, automated technology support. The scope of the challenge requires addressing it from both sides: widening the funnel and filling the pipeline to fill demand from one direction, and from the other side, reducing the amount of work and the level of expertise required to maintain robust defenses, intelligent monitoring, and agile incident response. No matter how it is achieved, closing the gap between supply and demand is imperative for an enterprise to develop an effective security posture — and on a larger scale, critical to maintaining public trust and reliable public and commercial services.

If the pool of applicants at a certain level of skill, qualification, and experience is so small that most organizations (including SMEs, government agencies, and municipal services) can't afford to hire any of the available candidates, something is fundamentally dysfunctional about the job market. Moreover, talented security staff are in such high demand, even if you manage to hire a choice candidate, that they may soon be lured away by better perks and projects at more a more prestigious organization. Thus, the gridlock we find ourselves in at present. By making reasonable adjustments to requirements for levels of education, certifications, and years of experience, companies and industries can loosen the jam and fill up their talent pool.

The delta between security job openings and qualified candidates isn't inevitable. For many organizations, it could be as simple as encouraging hiring managers to be more flexible and developing more informed and imaginative recruitment and apprenticeship practices.

FUTURE: WORKING TOWARD HUMAN-CENTRIC SECURITY

Many promising candidates, including recent graduates, are interested in high-tech companies and careers, but information security is perceived as deeply technical (and let's be honest, also tedious and high stress), leaving recruiters struggling to connect with candidates from less specialized backgrounds.

Smart leaders are swiftly recognizing that bright, diligent, inquisitive individuals are among the most valuable security assets an enterprise can leverage. A human-centric approach to information security will foster a workforce that can meet the challenges presented by digital risk — not to mention technology solutions that free up human resources and reduce tedium and complexity.

A human-centric approach provides the framework for building a balanced, fully staffed security workforce of proficient and satisfied information security professionals. Of course, this approach requires leadership commitment and budget allocation — but it's a crucial investment in the future. And in cyber security, the future comes at you fast.

CLOSING THE GAP BETWEEN SUPPLY AND DEMAND

Closing the gap between supply and demand is imperative for an enterprise to develop an effective security posture. It is evident that individuals with the required skills, qualifications and experience are either unavailable or demanding compensation that cannot be met with existing budgets. Because they are in high demand, talented security staff regularly move to new employers as they seek out better salaries and projects at more prestigious companies.

But is this inevitable? Are hiring managers so inflexible in requiring candidates to have specific skills, qualifications, and years of experience that they end up hindering their security teams? Are uninformed and unimaginative recruitment practices contributing significantly to the perceived shortage? As salaries escalate, organizations are urgently seeking a solution to the perceived crisis around hiring security professionals.

To address the growing demand, organizations need to broaden their approach, and work purposefully to recruit security professionals from a diversity of backgrounds, disciplines and skill sets. Focus on the aptitude and attitude of candidates rather than insisting on a host of specific skills, experience and qualifications that eliminate a large portion of current and prospective information security professionals.

BRIDGING THE DIVIDE: LEVERAGING HUMAN RESOURCES (HR)

Many security workforces experience a disconnect with HR, often due to HR misunderstanding the complexity and scale of demands on these teams. This hinders the organization's ability to identify relevant talent and provide adequate support for the professional development of existing employees. To bridge the divide, the information security function needs to adopt a series of well-established HR concepts.

These HR concepts – united under workforce planning, including a competency framework and workforce management – have been successfully embedded across most business functions and can be leveraged to address challenges related to the security workforce. Security leaders should foster a close relationship with HR to ensure these concepts are effectively embedded. It is fundamental for relevant functions responsible for information security – either entirely or in part – to take direct ownership of workforce planning, competency framework and workforce management concepts in order to build a sustainable security workforce prepared for the future.

WORKFORCE PLANNING:

To help manage personnel, organizations should adopt a concept known as workforce planning. This practice focuses on delivering a plan that incorporates short and long-term organizational objectives for personnel.

A conventional workforce planning cycle comprises five stages that can be leveraged to plan, build and maintain a security workforce that sustainably and effectively supports organizational and functional objectives. Workforce planning can be adopted directly by security leaders in conjunction with input from HR and business managers across the organization. Workforce planning helps articulate and identify solutions for many of the challenges being faced by the security workforce. Additionally, workforce planning is a highly valuable exercise, making an organization and function aware of risks in the security workforce, developing plans to overcome such risks, and focusing on meeting organizational objectives.

Most organizations have an unstructured or tactical approach to workforce planning within information security:

- An unstructured approach mainly comprises ad hoc recruitment, for someone matching a previous job occupant, as and when required.
- A tactical approach focuses on elements of workforce planning, such as using a competency framework to aid professional development.

More mature organizations have adopted strategic workforce planning, which involves integrating the security workforce with the relevant function's strategy, aligning skills, roles and people to fulfil short and long-term objectives.

COMPETENCY FRAMEWORK:

A competency framework forms a component of workforce planning, defining the knowledge, skills and attributes needed for individuals within the organization. It can be used to create a profile for each role required to achieve the security workforce's objectives. These roles and accompanying competencies will help shape many workforce planning and management activities.

While less than half of ISF Members use a competency framework to assess the skills and capabilities of professionals in the security workforce, there is a growing willingness, with more than 80% declaring in a recent ISF survey that they would consider either adopting an in-house developed version or drawing on an existing competency framework specific to cyber security for their security workforce. Many mature organizations develop a bespoke competency framework appropriate for their specific environment.

WORKFORCE MANAGEMENT:

Workforce management, sometimes referred to as talent management, forms another component of workforce planning, ensuring the functional objectives set out in the workforce plan are delivered successfully by employees and contractors, in alignment with organization objectives. It incorporates the development and retention of employees, focusing on areas such as career paths, performance management and rotation programs. Aligned with a role profile and corresponding competencies, workforce management enables individuals to work with their team and manager to develop their skills and experience in accordance with their career and personal aspirations. However, organizations should expect a degree of attrition as long-term partnership between employee and employer diminishes. Gone are the days where the majority of employees are seeking a job for life — most professionals are seeking to build a richer portfolio of careers.

Strategies like performance management programmes, which can include regular appraisals to assess performance and identify development opportunities, are the most widely adopted by our members. However, more than 60% of recently surveyed ISF Members have undefined career paths in information security. Used effectively, workforce management in information security can help organizations address unstructured roles and prevent employees moving elsewhere in pursuit of career development.

Organizational engagement with employees is fundamental to effective workforce management. While employee engagement methods vary between organizations, common themes include:

- Providing strong organizational or functional leadership
- Articulating objectives clearly
- Coaching and developing individuals by managers who mentor
- Encouraging employees to contribute and collaborate with the wider workforce
- Delivering organizational or functional integrity and maintaining transparency with employees

Moving forward, organizations need to establish a series of strategic objectives that lay a foundation for a stronger workforce and more robust pipeline. With clear direction and sustained HR efforts, organizations can formalize the structure of the security workforce, harness the appropriate talent, and bring security teams into better alignment with the organization's security objectives.

As the security workforce matures and finds innovative ways to embrace the vast resources of untapped talent, the exaggerated myth of a looming crisis in the global security workforce should reshape into a more realistic picture of the challenges ahead, making room for innovation and wider adoption of proven strategies and best practices. A robust and diverse security workforce will empower organizations to face future workforce challenges, such as automation, role and function amalgamation, and increased outsourcing. ISF Members are already demonstrating success at cultivating teams with the necessary skills and expertise in progressive and engaging environments.

THE IMPERATIVE OF A SUSTAINABLE SECURITY WORKFORCE

Our deepening reliance on connected digital systems, and our subsequent vulnerability to a shifting array of cyber threats, has made the security workforce core to enterprise profitability and survival. But for many enterprises, developing a sustainable security workforce is out of reach because attracting and retaining experienced, certified security experts is a constant battle. To break this impasse, governments, industries and companies need to establish strategic objectives that prioritize transformative investments in developing a stronger workforce and a bigger, more accessible talent pool.

A sustainable security workforce is essential if the information security function is to become a partner to the business and effectively manage the increasing cyber risk and security burden. With clear direction and sustained HR efforts, organizations can formalize the structure of security teams, reporting, and leadership to bring them into better alignment with the organization's security objectives. An integrated, agile security function can be a powerful partner to the business.

In the bigger picture, the more stakeholders work together towards the common goal of diversifying, growing, and advancing the security workforce, the safer shared cyberspace will be. In large part, our digital world runs on shared data and networks and relies on the public's trust. Security professionals are the guardians of these assets. In the year ahead, rise above the hiring fray and focus on fresh, strategic, long-term approaches to building, supporting, and integrating your security workforce.

13

THE IMPORTANCE OF CREATING THE RIGHT WORK CULTURE

CHRIS PINDER, IASME CONSORTIUM LTD

"In the fight against cyber-crime, employees can be an organisation's greatest asset or its biggest weakness." It's a perfectly logical statement frequently paraphrased at seminars delivering practical guidance on countering the cyber threat. By embracing this assertion, staff really can be one of *the* most effective tools; however, for the proclamation to be truly effective, just as with any other aspect of our job roles, employees need to be provided with the right support.

Utopia would be for all employees to effortlessly integrate cyber safe practices into their everyday work environment. The reality, unfortunately, is somewhat different. It is a safe assumption that the majority of the employed population are unaware of the true ramifications of cyber crime and, therefore, remain innocently unaware that their own actions can, positively or negatively, directly impact their employer's security. To encourage staff to think and act cyber secure, it could be argued that culture is a key tool necessary to enable a cyber secure environment.

The definitions for business culture are numerous. For simplicity, in this chapter, we are essentially talking about expressing an organisation's ethos in relation to risk and improved resilience. The agreed culture can impact how a company is viewed externally; it can impact how employees act internally. Yet, culture is much more than mere words; it is also the actions taken. Well intended words are meaningless unless they are backed up by solid actions. To help deliver the preferred culture, therefore, the complimentary support of governance, communication and training are fundamental. For clarity, when we reference governance in this context, we are referring to the action or manner of governing an organisation; its policies, procedures, processes etc.

THE REAL BUSINESS RISKS

Cyber security is a very real business risk. The National Cyber Security Centre encourages businesses to assume that the probability of an attempted attack taking place is 'when' not 'if'. Despite this stark warning, in the main, the cyber risk is not given the primacy it warrants. All too often cyber security is considered an inconvenience, an expense, an unwanted distraction. In reality, the real inconvenience, expense and distraction comes once an incident actually occurs. Prevention really can be far cheaper than the cure! Until a business starts to fully appreciate the unquestionable risk that the cyber threat presents, it will be challenging to implement any culture which is appropriate and proportionate to the organisation's risk.

THE ROLE THAT STAFF CAN PLAY

Many general business management manuals will reference the importance of 'leading from the top'. In terms of setting the right cyber secure culture, this well used adage is very apt. Regardless of a business size, a leadership that appreciates the significance of the cyber threat, its potential impact and the role employees can play, is the business that sets the foundations for a solid resilience.

Few businesses will perceive how their accounting team, their marketeers, their field ops and many other positions increase the exposure to the cyber threat. The accounting personnel, for example, may be vulnerable to invoice fraud, the marketeers may be subject to clicking fraudulent links on social media, field ops may be open to exposing or losing sensitive data (employers' and clients' data) and so the list goes on. Despite all this, the job responsibilities of the vast majority of today's work force do not incorporate cyber security considerations. For most, it is not seen as relevant. For the mainstream, it is certainly not seen as a discipline of interest. To the majority of the workforce, the perception is that the solutions required to protect a business are technical and therefore must be the responsibility of the IT team. Few see it as it should be i.e. the responsibility of everyone. Mention cyber security to most employees and the traditional preconceptions spring to mind: it's too complex; it's too sophisticated; there's nothing I can do about it; it will never happen to me. All common excuses or, given the increase in both the frequency and complexity of cyberattacks, maybe it's better to label these as unfortunate *misconceptions*.

Of course, many of the solutions required for improved security are technically based and will require the know-how of those who specialise in this field or have a good working knowledge. However, some very simple yet effective measures do not take much time, expense or resource. For example, how time consuming and costly is it to come up with a strong password? Using the guidance from the National Cyber Security Centre we should build our passwords using three random words; an amalgam that a good friend would not be able to guess in 20 attempts. Yet how many employees still use 'password', 'qwerty', '12345678'? The cyber criminals are all too aware that many people still use these basic passwords, so a simple requirement for staff to 'think strong passwords' can in itself be a significant first step.

Businesses, especially SMEs, face many demands on precious and limited time. It takes significant effort to juggle all the balls necessary to run a business or to carry out a job role in line with the expectations of our employers. Any new responsibilities to be taken on board, such as being cyber aware, have to be seen as more pressing than matters already on our existing hectic agendas. It is hardly surprising, therefore, that there is a reluctance to take on any further training or responsibility, especially if we cannot readily see how it relates to the business or the job role. For cyber security to compete, firstly it has to be seen as important to the business. The business in turn has to filter that thinking throughout the organisation; top down and bottom up. Only then can the business fully expect the whole organisation to implement and respect measures which are proportionate and appropriate to the respective risk of that company.

GOOD COMMUNICATION IS KEY

Handled correctly, a cyber aware culture, backed up with appropriate training, clear communication and good governance, can help engage staff in meeting the over-arching objective of maintaining a business which is resilient to the cyber threats. Handled incorrectly, its effectiveness is limited. The following real-life examples help outline this.

In terms of their approach to cyber security, XYZ Ltd, name changed for purposes of anonymity, had some commendable governance in place in the form of policies designed to encourage good cyber safe practices. As a minimum their Governance, on paper at least, demonstrated good intentions. One such policy related to removable media. Removable media, such as USB sticks, can be a means by which cyber criminals spread malicious viruses. The malware is encoded in the USB and is set free when inserted into, for example, laptops. At the time of this particular scenario, USB sticks were common freebies regularly distributed at events and exhibitions.

XYZ Ltd had a very sensible policy stipulating that any staff receiving a USB stick must hand the device into the IT department before subsequent use within any work devices. The intention of the policy author was that the USB sticks would be checked for viruses before insertion in any of the company computers. In theory, an excellent approach.

For a while, all staff adhered to the policy. USB sticks were submitted to the IT team as required; however, once there, they then went into a blackhole for approximately four weeks before reappearing on the respective employee's desk. The time delay of circa a month started to cause inconvenience. These USB sticks contained copies of slides from presentations staff had attended, they contained product information of potential suppliers or they had spare capacity for staff to save some of their own presentations or documents. Consequently, the frustration of the time delay started to become inconvenient. XYZ's staff slowly but surely started to ignore the policy, bypass the IT team and plug the devices straight into their own computers or laptops. And that was *all* staff including the directors, the CEO and the Chairman. If the directors can do it, why can't anyone else!

For XYZ Ltd, the intention of encouraging a cyber safe culture through policies which fostered positive actions was admiral. The weakness in this scenario was communication. The perception amongst the unknowing staff was 'what harm could a little USB stick do? It only contains copies of slides so what could possibly go wrong!' None of the staff had an awareness of the potential detrimental consequences their innocuous looking USB stick could have on their employer's security. The cyber security risk simply did not enter their thinking. They were not the IT team; they were sales, marketing, accounts, admin. So, without the education and communication piece, then why should/ would it cross their minds?

Although staff were aware of the actual policy, no one knew of the rationale behind the policy. Here, XYZ had good governance but it was in isolation of the communication or training that made the words have relevance or meaning. The potential risks of using an unchecked USB had simply not been explained to the staff as a whole. Had it been communicated, all staff would have exercised patience and been perfectly willing to wait 4 weeks for the return of their USB. The staff's innocence, and I use *innocence* over *ignorance*, meant that collectively, they changed from being cyber guardians to a hacker's friend within a matter of months.

Sadly, examples like this are far from isolated. ABC Ltd, again, the name has been changed to maintain anonymity, is a company which also had very sensible policies in place to mitigate their exposure to risk. In this case, the example policy was one of not permitting staff to connect their own devices such as mobiles to the company wi-fi. This policy sensibly sought to prevent employees own personal devices from being a weak point on the corporate network. As in the XYZ Ltd example, the practicalities of adhering to this policy proved an inconvenience to some staff who didn't understand why such a practice was not permitted; they did not appreciate the risk. The staff *needed* to connect to the company Wi-Fi to check their WhatsApp messages, check their Facebook updates and, of course, do their shopping! A significant number of staff decided, unilaterally, that it was OK to flaunt the policies and access company wi-fi via their own devices. As in the first example, the reason for the breakdown was communication. Again, all staff knew of the policy, yet the reasons behind the policy were not communicated. Whilst the respective policies of XYZ Ltd and ABC Ltd made perfect sense to the Quality and IT teams, the reasons and risks had not been explained to the staff who subsequently found the corresponding policies a hindrance.

Whilst clearer communication would have addressed the issues raised in the examples above, it should be accepted that inadvertent mistakes will happen. Mistakes don't make people bad employees. A member of staff may innocently click on a link within a phishing email or the accounts team may receive a convincing email and forward money to a supplier who has allegedly changed their bank details. In such circumstances, setting the right culture can also influence how employees react in the interests of the business. Threats, be they actual or suspected, need to be reported at the earliest possible opportunity. The sooner a suspicious incident is reported, the sooner it can be investigated, addressed and mitigated. A no blame culture encourages staff to come forward. A culture of fear, however, can mean incidents may, at best, be reported with a delay, at worst, remain unreported. Having said that, there has to be a balance. Repeat offenders for example may need additional training or a firmer approach. Each individual company is best placed to understand the balance most relevant for their own employees.

Setting the right tone for a cyber secure culture can be established from an employee's first day. Basic initial training, explaining appropriate policies and outlining the business expectations can all be incorporated in to induction training in same way as, for example, health and safety. Explaining that risk is taken seriously throughout the organisation and that each individual has an important role to play in keeping the company safe helps clarify expectations.

GOOD PRACTICE

Many SMEs may not have a dedicated IT team, preferring instead to contract out their IT requirements. Regardless of whether the IT team is directly employed or not, there is value in assigning responsibility for cyber security to a designated individual within an organisation to help ensure that the cause is properly addressed. The responsible person doesn't necessarily have to carry out all the actions but must ensure all the actions are carried out. The chosen *co-ordinator* therefore, should be someone with relevant competence or at least given the training to assume competence.

Just like formal or informal quality management systems, cyber and risk management controls can be integrated as a natural part of daily business activities. Some simple measures such as setting screens to sleep when away from the desk may require thought at first yet soon become habit.

For good ideas on what useful measures to implement, the government backed Cyber Essentials scheme is a very effective start point. Cyber Essentials is aimed at encouraging businesses to implement the basic yet effective controls. The scheme itself focuses on the 5 core technical controls that, unaddressed, have been found to be the root cause of the majority of successful online attacks. By following the requirements of Cyber Essentials and through effective guidance available via the National Cyber Security Centre (www.ncsc.gov.uk), businesses of all sizes can start to implement habit forming good practice which in turn leads to greatly improved resilience.

IASME Governance is another good standard to consider and incorporates Cyber Essentials. Through the inclusion of good governance practices, IASME Governance compliments and builds on the technical controls of Cyber Essentials. Both Cyber Essentials and IASME Governance are written for the business community, yet, many of the principles are just as applicable to individuals in their daily lives. If these certifications are something your business has gone, or is going through, then share the good practice with your staff. It will arm them with good practice thus making them more secure in their home lives plus, if they are practising safe cyber at home, they are more likely to naturally bring those good habits back into the work environment.

THE BENEFITS OF A GOOD CULTURE

A good culture supported by governance, training and communication can make a difference between a business remaining secure or becoming yet another cyber-crime statistic. There are however, other advantages to a proactive approach to cyber security. Implementing the right measures, especially if proven through certifications like Cyber Essentials, IASME Governance or ISO27001, can help a business gain and retain business contracts. For example, many Government tenders require suppliers to evidence they have good security and, therefore, request the likes of Cyber Essentials as a pre-requisite of the tender. This is gathering momentum in the private sector too as more and more businesses actively encourage suppliers to prove the cyber security credentials their suppliers have in place. As suppliers represent a potential weak link, the integrity of a supply chain becomes increasingly important. And if that is not incentive enough, then consider the legal obligations. Article 5, Principal 6, of the General Data Protection Regulation, the so-called security principle, requires "security of data…using appropriate technical and organisational measures." i.e. the inclusion of cyber security.

Be it the result of a targeted attack or a general attack focusing on vulnerabilities, all too many businesses who previously felt that cyber security was irrelevant to their business, found out to their cost how wrong they were. Creating the right culture could protect against the significant time and cost associated of becoming a victim. The creation of a cyber secure culture will not be quick and like all journeys it will have a few twists and turns along the road. It is, however, a worthwhile journey creating improved resilience with every step.

14

REVIEWING AND UPDATING CONTINGENCY PLANS

RICHARD PREECE, ORKAS

So you have read this book, taken notes and applied the advice to the context of your business. Surely, job done and time to start getting back to the real business of business, growth and return on investment. Alas, to paraphrase, no plan survives contact with the enemy, or in this case: the changing nature of your business and its dependencies, threats and hazards from malicious and non-malicious cyber-incidents and the latent and new vulnerabilities created by people, processes and technology.

This is the reality of the complex *systems of systems* and hyper-connectivity that the interaction of people, technology and data create, otherwise known as cyber-space or digitisation. The result is a case of *when* and not *if* a cyber based incident will take place. If it can go wrong, it probably will go wrong, not always in the way predicted and often at the least opportune time. Due to the increasing amount of a company's value being derived from cyber-space, it can lead to an amplifier effect beyond the initial incident, placing greater importance upon consequence management.

By way of simple analogy there is a *system of systems*, creating a capability for fire based risks, which covers: culture, people, policies, plans, processes, structures, information, technology and physical assets. These are linked into protective, preventative, detective, responsive and recovery measures and controls. For example, trained people ready to use fire extinguishers, alarms, muster points, calling the fire brigade, fire-insurance, forensic investigation, etc. This system of systems has developed over centuries of hard-earned experience.

So what; the fiduciary duties of the top management of companies make it increasingly unacceptable not to have the same approach for cyber-risks. In reality this means investing in planning, resourcing, budgeting and implementing a portfolio of programmes, projects and activities to review, continuously improve and change capability. This includes a team and contingency plans that are designed and prepared to be agile, so they can operate effectively against a range of potential scenarios in a complex, uncertain and ambiguous environment.

For some organisations, this approach may be a natural extension of their culture and current practices, for others it may be new and challenging. Done properly the business can become more agile and resilient, ready to mitigate the risks and seize the opportunities of cyber-space. However, done badly it can suffer material impact and even existential threat to its survival.

The aim of this chapter is therefore to provide a framework for any business to govern, invest in, review and update scenario based contingency plans, so they stay effective and efficient. This will be achieved by identifying a simple set of core questions to be addressed. From this will lead to the types of activities that need to be done and therefore built into your company's operating model. At the heart of this approach is the acceptance that cyber-incidents (malicious and non-malicious) are a case of *when* and not *if*.

WHERE TO START – WITH THE END IN MIND

Stephen Covey identified the importance of starting with the end in mind and so it is for cyber-incidents. There are really three questions that top management need to answer and to continue to ask:

1. Business growth and return on investment – do we understand where our value is and what the cyber-risk (including opportunity) is to it?;
2. Could we defend our level of preparation and response in the aftermath of a cyberincident?; and
3. Has the situation changed?

These simple questions help top management to provide strategic alignment, leadership and culture, governance and accountability. In turn, this should lead to prioritised and ongoing resourced risk management and capability. So having posed the questions, how to answer them?

Business growth and return on investment – do we understand where our value is and what the cyber-risk is to it? To answer this question requires an understanding of context and how the business creates value first, both now and under future plans. There are many tools and techniques that can be used and applied. However, scenario and contingency planning requires leadership and culture first and foremost to be ready to challenge one another and themselves and to be clear on what is known, what is assumed, what is unknown, but can be discovered and accepting that some things will be unknowable.

Whether starting from a mature understanding or from nothing, the simplest approach is for top management to use a facilitated workshop to develop shared understanding and agreement, with a particular focus upon cyber-space. This type of activity can focus upon how value is created, in particular how cyber-space allows the company to do things better, and to do better things. For example, through increased productivity and asset utilisation; more responsive and efficient supply chains and logistics; by improving customer and employee engagement; and, or some other form, innovation. Ultimately, this should create insights into how cyber-space enables faster, better and cheaper ways for people to people (P2P); people to machine (P2M) and machine to machine (M2M) to interact and exploit information and data.

This first activity allows more strategic evaluation of what is most important to, and needs to be prioritised by, the business. This can create new insights which can be beneficial to the business as a whole, highlighting dependencies and connections which may have grown organically over time, creating a self-organised criticality. For top management it can aid their ability to understand and lead overall business strategy and execution, enabling them to make better informed trade-off judgements between opportunities and risks.

This leads to the second stage in addressing this question – to understand the risk to the value the business creates, building upon the understanding already created and developing analysis of the insights further. This can and increasingly does include the significant risk of not digitally transforming to keep up with new or existing competition, or to innovate. This in turn enables an understanding of business impact of different scenarios upon P2P, P2M, M2M and enabling data will be on the company's reputation and brand; people and stakeholders; operations and supply-chain; legal and regulatory compliance; and financial and commercial outputs, including future investability. This process therefore provides the understanding to evaluate, direct, monitor and assure strategy, risk management and investment tradeoffs. It is already done by many businesses in one form or other of strategy and risk management activities. Cyber-space strategy and risks should be no different, but it is more challenging because of the complex, dynamic and ambiguous environment, cutting across traditional functional stovepipes and linkages outside the control of the company.

This analysis can then lead to the conduct of specific cyber-risk scenario events: workshops, table-top exercises and simulations, as appropriate. Scenarios should be developed which reflect the assessed threat and vulnerabilities to your company, both malicious and non-malicious, people and technically based. The events should have clear aims and objectives and most importantly, the ability to capture observations and conduct analysis to identify lessons and recommendations. These can then inform wider governance, risk management and specific contingency plans.

When preparing for, conducting and assessing the results of these cyber-risk scenario events, it is important that the most likely and most dangerous types of threats and hazards are considered as a priority. Individuals and parts of the company may find this challenging based upon past experience, assumptions and cultural norms. Perhaps the two most challenging aspects of this are for those with a non-technical background to engage with the subject matter, and recognise the human dimension, especially that of the threat posed by the malicious insider. To counter this, an education package to understand the wider issues and risks is recommended before the scenario events. Equally, there needs to be clear rules of engagement, so any discussion and debate is free and open, with the event seen as an opportunity to learn first and foremost; making mistakes and problem solving as appropriate.

The aim of these activities is to enable shared understanding and discovery driven learning, whilst improving collaboration across different functions, including potentially with external stakeholders. Many of these cyber-risk scenario activities will identify areas for measures to improve prevent, protect, and detect. The results from these events can therefore support more integrated decision making, including some of the inevitable trade-offs required to achieve strategic alignment. This leads to the strategic second question and, with it, having a view of what good looks like!

What Does Good Look Like? US Supreme Court Justice Potter Stewart famously said, "I know it when I see it" when he described the threshold test for obscenity. So it is when attempting to define what good looks like to defend a business's preparation and response to cyber-incidents. So how will you answer the second strategic question?

Could we defend our level of preparation and response in the aftermath of a cyber-incident? The first step of this has been achieved by conducting the analysis and scenario events described above, which should help identify criticality and priority for protecting different assets and value, both tangible and intangible. However, having identified value and the criticality and priority of different cyber-space assets in achieving value, it is necessary to consider the what if something has an impact upon achieving value.

This means developing, practising and testing contingency plans to demonstrate they are more than mere arrangements, but fit for purpose and ready to be used. In practice this means developing an agile core multi-disciplinary team, which can bring in others as required, to dynamically problem solve and execute solutions under pressure. This team, including accountable members from top management, need stable core processes and structures that can enable rapid mobilisation and action across a range of functions.

There are, therefore, a further two questions to ask of the contingency plans as they are first developed and subsequently practised, tested and continuously adapted. These questions are:

2a. How will we detect and recognise a malicious or non-malicious cyber-incident? The nature of many cyber-scenarios is that attribution and the time of the initial occurrence of an event and its first detection can be challenging. This means the initial assessment and reporting of an event to an appropriate authority can be delayed. So the contingency plan must have a clear policy, process, people and structure, including outsourced services if appropriate, and supporting technologies, infrastructure, information and intelligence, to make this as efficient and effective as possible. This may enable proactive actions to prevent an attack or failure of some sort or to quickly contain it. However, it is more likely to be in response to an incident having being detected, possibly through information released publicly or on the dark web. A cyber-incident contingency plan timeline and actions should therefore look something like the framework in Figure 5.5.1.

Figure 5.5.1 Generic Contingency Plan Framework

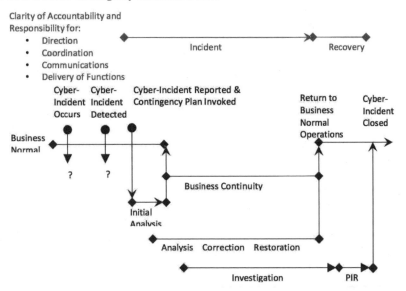

2b. Is the decision making and action process effective and ensures effective communications to stakeholders including for 2nd and 3rd order consequences? This should be a core part of any contingency plan; it is informed by the assessment of what the incident is, but considers what the likely consequences are. The subsequent incident categorisation, which may change during an incident, should determine who has delegated responsibility for direction, coordination, action and communications.

Figure 5.5.2 Generic Incident Categorisation Framework

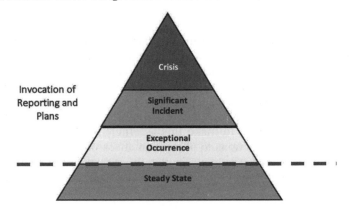

The generic incident categorisation framework in Figure 5.5.2 is a guide, but the key is to keep it simple and enable agility in execution. Any incident assessed to fit above the red dashed line should result in immediate reporting as a minimum. However, in reality there will be a routine amount of attacks and activity, which the cybersecurity function should understand; these should have little or no business impact and be treated as business as usual. Therefore, top management should direct what is the agreed tolerance of business impact for reporting and who should be responsible, consulted and informed, depending upon the categorisation of the incident. Ultimately a member of the top management should be accountable and ready to lead and direct the overall strategic response to a significant incident and especially a crisis.

If scenario and contingency planning have been effective, it should identify who, both internally and externally to the business, should be informed. This should be included within an incident management communications plan, which should capture what will be communicated, when it will be communicated, with whom, and how; plus any non-disclosure agreements or other caveats/factors to information sharing. This is particularly important in the event of a special investigation, often revolving around a potential malicious insider threat. Lawyers and communications specialists should help shape this plan. Stakeholders who should be considered in the plan include: employees, customers, suppliers, regulators, law enforcement, cyber information sharing portals, legal, insurance and other incident/crisis management service providers.

PULLING IT ALL TOGETHER

Cybersecurity and contingency planning is not simple; however, it must be done, if the fiduciary duties of the top management are to be satisfied. Therefore, it should be viewed as an essential core and ongoing business process for companies. How it is done must be driven by the top management, who must own and lead the issues and risks, although education and culture should make it everyone's responsibility to play their part. The key is to continually be ready to ask question 3.

Has the situation changed? Ultimately contingency plans should be kept simple and have the agility to be applied to not just specific named scenarios or likely start points, but also the unexpected. They should be living documents, regularly updated following Post Incident Reviews (PIR), other organisations' lessons, development and test exercises, changes in strategy, risk appetite, personnel, technology, suppliers, intelligence and operations.

The key is to continually question assumptions and the situation. The hyperconnected (P2P, P2M and M2M) environment, in which small events can be magnified in terms of impact, means the situation is continually in flux and therefore changing. This requires a commitment, with supporting governance and accountability, risk management, leadership and culture, and agile capabilities to continually deepen and broaden individual and shared understanding of the issues and risks and to adapt. The iterative design and development review process should build upon existing company culture and processes if they already exist. As in so many things the challenge is to have sufficient detail to make the contingency plan(s) work, but not so much that it is overly prescriptive and not fit for purpose when it comes into contact with the enemy.

15

THE COST OF A CYBER INCIDENT

THE UNEXPECTED SOCIAL AND FINANCIAL IMPACTS FOLLOWING A BREACH

VIJAY RATHOUR, GRANT THORNTON, DIGITAL FORENSICS GROUP

"I am convinced that there are only two types of companies: those that have been hacked and those that will be. And even they are converging into one category: companies that have been hacked and will be hacked again."

Robert S. Mueller, III
Federal Bureau of Investigation

It is received wisdom that if you operate a computer environment that is connected to the internet, you will be a target of cyber attackers. Indeed, you probably already have been. Our analysis and observations have confirmed reports[1] that a computer newly connected to the internet will come under attack and be probed for improper access within five minutes – day or night, every day of the year. And these timelines only promise to get tighter: connected cameras, smartwatches, mobile phones and 5G self-driving cars are all attractive targets for malicious attacks.

We live in a connected world and increasingly those we connect to are motivated by crime, vandalism, curiosity or political goals to undermine our cyber defences and

---

1. https://www.netscout.com/sites/default/files/2019-02/SECR_001_EN-1901%20-%20NET-SCOUT%20Threat%20Intelligence%20Report%202H%202018.pdf

use our property, physical and intellectual, to their advantage. Responding to these inevitable attacks requires an equally efficient, experienced and effective response from Computer Forensic experts. However, the social, psychological and emotional impacts following a cyber event are often overlooked and we have found that these can be at least as damaging as the financial impact following a cyber-attack.

WATER UNDER THE BRIDGE

Customers increasingly are on the receiving end of apologies and plaintive pleas for forgiveness from a business or service they have shared information with after they suffer the inevitable data breach. Those breaches often result in the loss of very personal, very sensitive and very valuable (to the customers) data; and it seems only natural to blame the business for failing to secure it adequately.

Ironically, the ubiquity of data breaches is becoming an increasingly valuable tool for a business devastated by a cyber-attack! "Notification fatigue" has blunted the novel pain of a breach of data for many customers as they increasingly lose confidence in the cyber-security of businesses they work with, or resign themselves to the inevitability of a breach. Recent studies indicate that most customers are suffering from an average of nearly two[2] breaches a day, whether known or unknown to them.

Inevitably, customer loyalty and confidence in a brand will be impacted following the admission by a business that it has fallen victim to a cyber-attack. Studies in the US have reported that 75% of potential and existing customers would not engage with a company that they felt did not respect their data[3], and most organisations that publicly report a cyber incident that has resulted in the loss of customer data will suffer immediate negative customer sentiment.

Despite this gloom, however, prompt and effective handling of the crisis can significantly shorten the financial impact, brand damage and interruption to business that can follow the attack. One of the most significant factors that will influence this recovery period is the *perceived* effectiveness of the business' response to the cyber-attack[4]. Surveys of major breaches over recent years have shown that the most impactful factor on reducing the long-term cost of a data breach is the creation and deployment of a team dedicated to effective resolution of the incident. Establishing an Incident Response Team resulted in an average reduction in financial harm of about 10% over the lifetime of the incident.

It is advisable for this Team to include the skills of Computer Forensic experts experienced in navigating the challenges of a cyber incident, alongside senior executives from within the business, and perhaps legal counsel, Public Relations and Communications experts, amongst others. This crisis team can focus on providing timely and effective actions aimed at containing the incident, both practically and from a reputational and PR perspective.

---

2. https://www.privacyrights.org/data-breaches

3. https://www.prnewswire.com/news-releases/new-survey-finds-deep-consumer-anxiety-over-data-privacy-and-security-300630067.html

4. https://www.ibm.com/security/data-breach

STRESS TESTING

Poor incident handling can cause immediate and longstanding damage to the business, but the skills required to handle a complex cyber incident may not be readily available to it.

Although we are focusing on the circumstances of a cyber-attack and its impact on the business, in our experience the cause of the incident can be a relatively minor detail in a broader factual tapestry – this is a **business crisis**, not just a cyber crisis. There are a myriad of technical details that may be relevant, such as attack vectors, categories of Personally Identifiable Information that have been lost, liability for emotional distress caused by exfiltration of data etc; the list goes on. But fundamentally, this is a crisis that requires the business to engage with its customers, its suppliers, its regulators, and itself.

Most businesses and their staff will have the good fortune of not having to suffer a business crisis, but with the inevitability of cyber-attacks it is highly advisable to plan for the realities of this crisis and prepare, practically and mentally, for the fallout.

Living through a cyber crisis can be exceptionally challenging for even the best prepared employee, and this is even before the public perception of the breach is factored in. Customers that are impacted by the loss of data caused by a cyber attack are right to regard themselves as a victim and invariably they will hold the business accountable for the loss.

In many cyber incidents the business can count itself amongst the victims as a crime has been committed and it has suffered as the target, and yet there will be little sympathy for an organisation that has under-invested in effective cyber-prevention, or executives that are ham-fisted in their response.

Law and precedent related to cyber-attacks continues to evolve, but courts and regulators around the world are prepared to appoint blame on businesses and staff that fail to respond with appropriate diligence to the incident. In the US a corporate may be held liable where there has been "a sustained or systematic failure of the board to exercise oversight"[5]. Large data breaches have allowed courts to entertain considerations around the frequency and adequacy of board and executive meetings to discuss cyber-security issues.

Delegation of responsibility to such a degree that the board or senior leadership have no effective insight and awareness of these issues is likely to attract the full severity of legal sanctions. These issues are coming even more starkly into focus with the spectre of 'class actions' for subjects of a data breach, direct responsibility and accountability for "senior managers" for cyber security issues[6], and shareholder and investor actions for failure by the corporate to respond appropriately.

---

5. https://www.casebriefs.com/blog/law/business-associations/business-associations-keyed-to-hamilton/duty-of-care-and-the-business-judgment-rule-business-associations-keyed-to-hamilton-business-associations-law/stone-v-ritter/
6. https://www.fca.org.uk/publication/corporate/applying-smr-to-fca.pdf

A HELPING HAND

A string of global corporate tragedies has encouraged regulators to assess the root causes that contributed to them, and opportunities to learn from them. Many organisations operate with well executed, audited and effective *operational* plans, but a far smaller number will focus on the development of a **crisis management strategy**. This gap has been one of the motivating drivers in the development of British Standard 11200:2014, *"Crisis Management – Guidance and Good Practice"*. Although this Standard is now supplemented by the more recent PD CEN/TS 17091:2018 *"Crisis Management – Building a Strategic Capability"*, the operating guidance that the Standard provides is instructive to all teams engaged in responding to an operational crisis, and not just those related to cyber incidents.

PD CEN/TS 17091 defines a crisis as an *"unprecedented or extraordinary event or situation that threatens an organisation and requires a strategic, adaptive, and timely response in order to preserve its viability and integrity"*.

The guidance contained within these documents help reinforce that crisis management is a **strategic** issue that must be addressed from the highest levels of the business downwards, rather than being ignored, considered haphazardly, or developed in silos.

BS 11200:2014 identifies core executive skill development areas including:

- Crisis management concepts and principles;
- Developing and building a crisis capability;
- Crisis leadership and decision making;
- Crisis communications; and
- Training, exercising and learning from crises.

In particular, it encourages the organisation to develop a crisis management lifecycle, illustrated in Fig. 15.1 below:

Figure 15.1 – The crisis management lifecycle

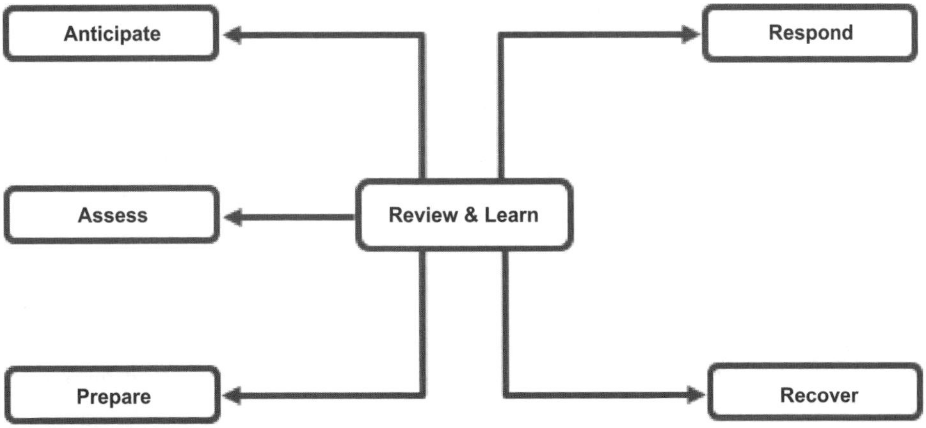

The guidance places at its centre a focus on **reviewing and learning** from previous crisis experience, through testing and validation of plans. Stemming from here businesses, and especially senior management, are encouraged to develop skills to **respond quickly** in an informed manner. This will support the goal of **recovering** from the crisis and moving into a "longer term, strategically directed effort to recover reputation and value".

These efforts will of course be supported by **anticipating** potential crises, **assessing** evidence to allow the business to make effective judgements about the actions required, and thus, **preparing** the organisation to face "specific risks and handle crises that are not foreseen".

WEATHERING THE STORM

Effective preparation for unforeseen events has been proven to help companies perform financially better than those that do not[7]. Indeed, some businesses have been able to "create value from a crisis" through effective management and leadership, and found that the valuation of their businesses have *increased* following a cyber incident by demonstrating that they have been tested and weathered the storm.

Lessons learned by these business show that:

- prevention is better than cure in responding rapidly to warnings of weaknesses within the business, particularly within the IT and cyber infrastructure;
- taking early and effective responsibility for the crisis will empower teams to be accountable but empowered to fix the problem;
- communicating with customers impacted by a cyber attack with respect and in the spirit of trust, not merely technical jargon, demonstrated an understanding of the customer's fear and frustration, and presented a "light at the end of the tunnel"; and
- a rapid response with effective "customer focused" remedial action will help address reputational harm.

It is inevitable that in the aftermath of a data breach or high visibility crisis a business will find itself under the microscope by customers, regulators, investors and law enforcement bodies. Ineffective management and evidence of a poor strategy in a crisis may therefore lead to investor and shareholder revolt, potentially even resulting in calls for a change of leadership.

CRISIS LEADERSHIP

Associated to the standards and guidance considered above, British Standard BS 31111:2018 *"Cyber risk and resilience. Guidance for the governing body and*

7. https://www.aon.com/getmedia/2882e8b3-2aa0-4726-9efa-005af9176496/Aon-Pentland-Analytics-Reputation-Report-2018-07-18.pdf

executive management" reinforces expectations on effective executive leadership in a cyber crisis.

Many executives tasked with responding to a cyber crisis will fail to prepare themselves for the significant mental and physical stress of responding to the incident. Inevitably, all notions of "business as usual" operations will be deprioritised as the business and its Incident Response Team focus on ***containing*** the crisis, ***identifying*** the root cause, and ***remediating*** the business from the impact of the attack[8].

Figure 15.2 – resolving the crisis

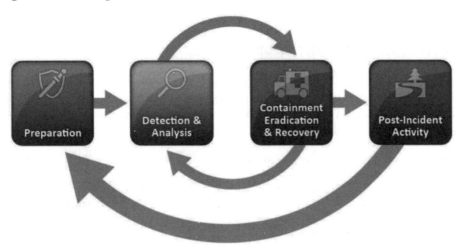

In our experience, a cyber-attack will require the CEO, Chief Security Office, Financial Director, General Counsel, Chief Technology Officer and others to dedicate almost their entire attention to resolution of the crisis, typically for days or weeks at a time. (See Fig. 15.2 above.) During this period, others in the business may be required to shoulder responsibilities they are unprepared for while the executive team is focused on the "new normal". Indeed, a successful resolution of the incident may depend on the senior management team's ability to ignore all other distractions by cocooning themselves in a "crisis centre."

BS 31111:2018 provides invaluable guidance for senior management teams to help familiarise them with the risks and requirements associated with developing effective cyber resilience. It seeks to establish good hygiene and best practises for boards and senior leadership, highlighting areas of focus during the crisis. These include consideration of internal and external risk factors, communication strategies with stakeholders inside and outside the business, culture and trust, and adaptability to rapidly changing circumstances as illustrated in Fig 15.3.

---

8. National Institute of Standards and Technology – Computer Security Incident Handling Guide: https://nvlpubs.nist.gov/nistpubs/SpecialPublications/NIST.SP.800-61r2.pdf

Figure 15.3 – Areas of focus during crisis

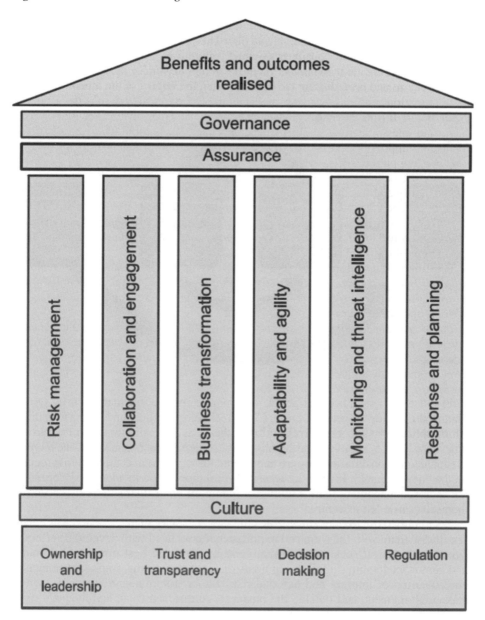

CRISIS COMMUNICATION

Addressing and pre-empting the needs of customers and external stakeholders can be critical to "righting the ship" following a crisis. The standards referred to above provide helpful guidance on the impact of the communication strategy following a cyber crisis.

Internal and external communication professionals can be invaluable in establishing the correct tone and candour in messaging, particularly in an age where any communication, public or private, will inevitably be repeated across the globe on social media. It is essential for businesses to plan and agree, in advance of the crisis, the form of messaging that senior-management can issue without incurring additional delays and approvals – time can be a critical factor and preparation helps prevent embarrassing public gaffes.

Addressing a 'social media storm' is a rapidly evolving art and may require skills not inherently comfortable for established senior executives in a business. The nature of the brand and the tone expected of it from its customers may also play a part: a blue-chip business may be expected to take the time to formulate a sombre and conservative reflection on the incident, while a start-up engaging with a youthful audience may regain brand loyalty through a "less varnished" tone.

Third-parties, including suppliers and financial markets, will require a more nuanced approach, with a particular focus on the legal and regulatory ramifications of formal statements. Underlying these concerns is the need for a ***strategic*** communication strategy, and not just a rush to fill the vacuum.

Those '*unprecedented or extraordinary events*' will invariably place staff under huge psychological stress, and a 'lighthouse in a storm', by way of plan of expected actions, independent experts to call upon, pre-planned financial tolerances, and communication tones to adopt, can all greatly alleviate the helpless that can otherwise infect the senior leadership, and thus inevitability all employees.

PLANNING FOR THE INEVITABLE

Organisations are advised to engage in cyber incident planning sessions to help prepare and practise for these inevitable incidents. These sessions can take a variety of forms, but at a minimum we strongly encourage organisations to ***repeat and reinforce*** learnings: a single benign table-top discussion annually is unlikely to reap significant improvements in behaviours. However, studies into cyber-security awareness and resilience have demonstrated that effective internalisation of best practises and awareness comes from repeated reinforcement of positive behaviours[9].

The SANS Institute, an internationally renowned training body specialising in cybersecurity awareness, illustrates this in its "**Security Awareness Maturity Model**" illustrated in Fig 15.4:

---

9. https://www.spiedigitallibrary.org/conference-proceedings-of-spie/11018/110180N/Long-lasting-effects-of-awareness-training-methods-on-reducing-overall/10.1117/12.2518934.short?SSO=1&tab=ArticleLink

Figure 15.4

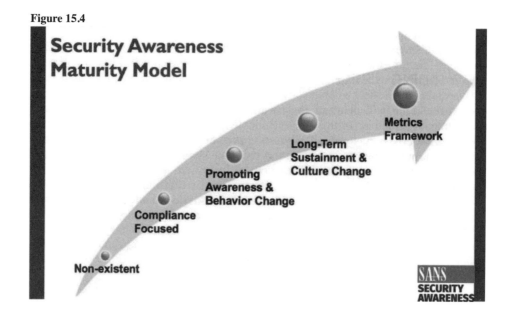

We recommend that organisations reflect internally, and potentially seek external support, in understanding their risk appetite, investment in cyber-security training and defence, and their posture during and following a cyber incident. This process should culminate in the preparation of an **Incident Response Plan**, a document designed to provide critical, concise and effective guidance in the circumstances of a crisis. Ideally it should **not** seek to provide too much detail as in our experience such plans rapidly become unwieldy and a hindrance rather than an aid.

After a plan is prepared it should be socialised at appropriate levels of detail across the organisation. Typically, the plan will designate by name and seniority the constitution of the **crisis response team**; this team should become familiar with the plan and be prepared to challenge it if they feel that it will not be beneficial or effective in a crisis. This stage of awareness will align with the middle of the SANS maturity model in 'promoting awareness and behaviour change'.

Despite these best efforts, however, in our experience of responding to cyber-attacks across a range of complexities and severities, we have observed that the Incident Response Plan, and perhaps associated Business Continuity Plans and dedicated Crisis Plans, will all fall by the wayside if the organisation fails to reinforce and practise them. 'Long-term sustainment and culture change' tends to be best exhibited by those organisations that test their plans at least once a year and we recommend that medium to large organisations should test their plans at least twice a year. This can take the form of a 'read-through' of the plan early in the year, updating provisions, contact details, communication trees and so on to ensure that it is contemporaneous. This exercise should then be followed up later in the year with a simulated cyber-attack that seeks to be as realistic as possible in 'stress testing' both the plan and the crisis-response team.

LIKE RIDING A BIKE

Cyber-attacks are inevitable and a business that fails to prepare for them is increasingly likely to be regarded as negligent or even liable for its own failures. Unprepared staff, faced with a crisis, may crumble under the pressure and contribute to even greater financial harm befalling the business, and gain little sympathy from the customers and secondary victims impacted by their actions.

However, despite these dark clouds, effective preparation and resilience can harden the business' resolve, arming staff with the mental fortitude and skills to find a way through these challenging times, bouncing back with vigour and lessons learnt for a brighter future.

ENDPIECE FROM CYBER AWARE

As the book outlines, it is our responsibility to take action to protect ourselves from hacking, bullying and to be cyber savvy. Some of the action needed is as simple as clicking on the privacy settings on our phone. We can all go take that extra effort to put simple security in place.

The government is a great source of information and a supporter for managing individual and business online security. CYBER AWARE (formerly Cyber Streetwise) is the government's first and only cyber security public awareness communications campaign delivering official and expert advice, based on the technical advice of the National Cyber Security Centre. CYBER AWARE aims to make good cyber security habits second nature, not an afterthought, for individuals and small businesses. Understanding and adopting simple online security is key to enabling individuals and small businesses to become more resilient against the cyber threat while also getting the most out of being online.

People are now connected from the moment they wake up to the moment they go to sleep – creating huge opportunities to integrate positive messaging on online security into online interactions be it with family, friends, clients or employees.

The impact of a cyber breach or attack can be huge: there's the time you could lose through having to fix your website or systems, the potential loss of customers, damage to your reputation and all the other potential consequences of a hacker getting their hands on your data. It's more important than ever to mobilise ourselves to provide this information consistently and coherently. CYBER AWARE is designed to do just this and supply key advice in the areas of,

Protecting Your Device – Software & Apps: https://www.cyberaware.gov.uk/software-updates

Security features: https://www.cyberaware.gov.uk/security-features

Protecting Your Data: – Passwords: https://www.cyberaware.gov.uk/passwords

Sharing Data: https://www.cyberaware.gov.uk/sharing-data

Back Up data: https://www.cyberaware.gov.uk/back-data

Protecting Your Business: – https://www.cyberaware.gov.uk/protect-your-business

Around a third of all businesses, 32% reported a cyber breach or attack in the past 12 months (*source: https://www.gov.uk/government/statistics/cyber-security-breaches-survey-2019*). The good news is protecting yourself from hackers and viruses does not have to take a lot of time, work or money. CYBER AWARE is encouraging the public and small businesses across the UK to do two simple things which can help improve their online security:

Conquer the Web

- Use a strong and separate password for your email (using three random words or numbers to create a strong password); hackers can use your email to access many of your personal accounts.
- Install the latest software and app updates; they contain vital security updates which help protect your device from viruses and hackers.

Once you put these two key actions in place, there are a range of Government-approved guidance you can follow to protect your business further.

- Cyber Essentials is an industry backed accreditation scheme for businesses, run by the Department for Culture, Digital, Media and Sport: https://www.cyberessentials.ncsc.gov.uk/
- Protect Your Data: https://ico.org.uk/for-organisations/business/
- Train Your Staff: https://www.gov.uk/government/collections/cyber-security-training-for-business
- If you are a small business and looking for more technical advice, please use the National Cyber Security Centre's Small Business Guide. https://www.ncsc.gov.uk/section/information-for/small-medium-sized-organisations

CYBER AWARE is supported by over 700 organisations, from law enforcement to major retailers, household brand names to charities and other Government departments, providing them with all the support and materials they need to communicate CYBER AWARE's advice in creative and innovative ways. If you would like to support the campaign, please get in touch with us at cyberaware@homeoffice.gov.uk.

CONTRIBUTORS' CONTACTS

AXELOS RESILIA
17 Rochester Row
London SW1P 1QT
Tel: +44 (0) 7860 950108
*Contact:*Nick Wilding
e-mail: Nick.Wilding@AXELOS.com

BeecherMadden
155 Fenchurch Street
London EC3M 6AL
Tel: +44 (0) 207 382 7980
Contact: Karla Reffold
e-mail: karla.reffold@beechermadden.com

Boolean Logical
20-22 Wenlock Road
London N1 7GU
Tel: +44 (0) 780 308 5249
Contact: Nick Ioannou
e-mail: nick@booleanlogical.com

CyberCare Ltd
Public Phone Line: 07496 955219
Contact: Maureen Kendal
e-mail: maureen@cybercare.org.uk

DLA Piper UK LLP
160 Aldersgate St
London EC1A 4AT
Rel: +44 (0) 20 7349 0296
Contact: Sam Millar
e-mail: sam.millar@dlapiper.com

Grant Thornton LLP
30 Finsbury Square
London EC2P 2YU
Tel: +4 (0) 207 184 4684
Contact: Vijay Rathour
e-mail: Vijay.Rathour@uk.gt.com

IASME Consortium Ltd
Wyche Innovation Centre
Upper Colwall
Malvern WR13 6PL
Contact: Chris Pinder
e-mail: chris.pinder@iasme.co.uk

Information Security Forum Ltd
10 Eastcheap
London EC3M 1AJ
Tel: +44 (0) 203 85 6909
e-mail: steve.durbin@securityforum.org

Richard Knowlton Associates Ltd
Office 10096
PO Box 6945
London W1A 6US
Tel: +44 (0) 7500 103164
     +39 (0) 3820 008 (Italy)
Contact: Richard Knowlton
e-mail: rk@rkassociates.eu

Legend Business Books Ltd
Legend Times Group
107-111 Fleet Street
London EC4A 2AB
Contacts: Tom Chalmers
Direct line: +44 (0) 207 9948
e-mail: tomchalmers@ legend-paperbooks.co.uk
Jonathan Reuvid
Tel: +44 (0) 1295 738070
e-mail: jonathan.reuvid@iprevents.com

Oakas Ltd
Richard Preece
Wessex House
Teign Road

Newton Abbot
Devon TQ12 4AA
Tel: +44 (0) 207 127 5312
Contact: Richard Preece
e-mail:Richard.Preece@oakas.co.uk

Penningtons Manches Cooper LLP
125 Wood Street
London EC2V 7AW
Tel:+44 (0) 20 7457 3000
Contact: Dan Hyde
e-mail: dan.hyde@penningtons.co.uk

Don Randall Associates
44 Fitzwalter Rd
Colchester
Essex CO3 3SX
Tel: +44 1206 767751
Contact: Don Randall
e-mail: donrandallassociates@gmail.com

Templar Executives Ltd
Contact: Chris Greany
e-mail: cjgreany@gmail.com

Think Cyber Security Ltd
Tel: +44 (0) 20 3151 8045
Contact: Tim Ward
e-mail: tim.ward@thinkcyber.co.uk

The University of Buckingham
Hunter Street
Buckingham MK18 1EG
Contact: Julian Richards
Tel: +44 (0) 1327 850391
e-mail: julian.richards@buckingham.ac.uk